89 HEIRLOOM RECIPES
FROM NEW YORK'S
MILK & COOKIES BAKERY

# MILK & COOKIES

by **Tina Casaceli**

Photographs by **Antonis Achilleos**

Written with **Judie Choate**

Foreword by **Jacques Torres**

CHRONICLE BOOKS
SAN FRANCISCO

Text copyright © 2011 by **Tina Casaceli**.

Photographs copyright © 2011
by **Antonis Achilleos**.

All rights reserved. No part of this book may
be reproduced in any form without written
permission from the publisher.

Library of Congress Cataloging-in-Publication
Data available.

ISBN 978-0-8118-7254-6

Manufactured in China.

Designed by **Vanessa Dina**.
Prop styling by **Pam Morris**.
Typesetting by **Janis Reed**.

Clark Bar is a registered trademark of New England
Confectionary Company. Frangelico is a registered
trademark of Giorgio Barbero and Figli, S.P.A. Kahlúa
is a registered trademark of The Kahlúa Co. M&M's is
a registered trademark of Mars, Inc. Nutella is a registered trademark of Ferrero S.P.A. Red Hots is a registered
trademark of Ferrara Pan Candy Company.

10 9 8 7 6 5 4 3 2 1

CHRONICLE BOOKS LLC
680 SECOND STREET
SAN FRANCISCO, CALIFORNIA 94107

WWW.CHRONICLEBOOKS.COM

# WITH APPRECIATION AND THANKS:

To my father, Norman, who loved good food as much as I do. Not a day goes by that his influence is not beside me. No experience or education can compare to the experience and education I gained as I grew up working with him; with my father, my strong foundations were built. I wouldn't be baking or running a business today nor, especially, writing a cookbook had he not taught me so well.

To my mother, Marilyn, for instilling the importance of family and keeping tradition in me. She always believed I could do whatever I put my mind to; I still find courage in that. I thank her also for having the patience and forethought to sit with our grandmothers — hers and mine — transcribing all of their recipes as they prepared them so the recipes would be passed down accurately. She neatly typed them and created a book of family recipes for me that I still have and use. Her thoughtfulness made writing the family chapter of this book a breeze.

To my brother, Phil, for always watching out for me. Having our businesses so close to each other has been a blessing; knowing he is just around the corner makes me feel secure. Watching him operate his business so flawlessly helped me believe I could do it, too. I especially thank him for providing lunch each day during the photo shoot for this book.

To my staff at Milk & Cookies Bakery, without whom there would be no Milk & Cookies Bakery. I especially thank Jennifer Tan, my pastry chef, who helped produce all the products needed for the photos in this book while never falling behind on any of the daily bakery production, and for dealing with my craziness and then laughing with me at the end of the day. Also to Jose Jerez, for bringing sunshine into our lives every day he walks through the bakery door!

To my friends Vicki Wells and Christopher Papagni, who understand when I don't have time to even grab a quick bite to eat with them, but who never stop asking.

Lisbeth Rawl, I thank you for our endless phone calls that always help me keep things in perspective.

To Sabena Singh, who has been another blessing in my life. There is no one like Sabena! My number-one fan, her encouragement and belief in me has helped me keep going.

To my friends and colleagues at The French Culinary Institute for their endless support and encouragement.

I am especially grateful to Judie Choate; she brought my idea from a thought to a reality. She makes it all seem so easy. There is no one better with whom one could write a book.

I am also grateful for my agent, Mickey Choate, who was the first to recognize the potential of this project and expertly guided me through the steps toward publication.

I would also like to thank my editors, Bill LeBlond and Sarah Billingsley, at Chronicle Books, for undertaking this project and offering their encouragement and wise words to make it the best it could possibly be. Also to Doug Ogan, Vanessa Dina, Tera Killip, Peter Perez, David Hawk, and all of the staff at Chronicle Books who deserve a huge thank you. You do a remarkable job and produce beautiful books.

My gratitude also goes out to Antonis Achilleos and Pam Morris for creating beautiful photos and never complaining as customers stepped over props and camera equipment during the entire photo shoot. You both have unbelievable patience and amazing talent.

A very special thank-you to Dave and Sue Pacelli and Bob Borreggine for the multiple weekends they spent driving down from Rochester, NY, sleeping on my apartment floor, and working all day and sometimes overnight to help me transform the bakery.

And finally, I would like to thank the many members of my extended family and my lifetime friends for their unconditional love and continuing support. Each of you has been with me all the way and, even though I don't mention you by name, I hope that you know who you are.

# MILK & COOKIES

### TABLE OF CONTENTS

# MILK & COOKIES

TABLE OF CONTENTS CONT'D

## CHAPTER 7
### FAMILY FAVORITES

## CHAPTER 8
### BROWNIES AND BARS

# FOREWORD
## BY JACQUES TORRES

In France, there is no such thing as "milk and cookies." A pot of tea, perhaps, and, of course, a dark espresso or warm café au lait each served with small biscuits or madeleines in the afternoon would be as close as you could get to the favorite American snack. In fact, I had never tasted a chocolate chip cookie until I came to the United States and now, not only do I make my own, you can frequently find me biking over to Milk & Cookies Bakery for one of Tina's just-like-homemade cookies for a midday pick-me-up.

I find that the extraordinary thing about all of the goodies at Milk & Cookies Bakery is that your childhood favorites taste even better than you remember! Tina Casaceli has taken all of her professional knowledge and pastry skills and combined them with the finest ingredients available to produce baked goods that are not only delicious but somehow also say "made with love," just like mom does at home. This is not easy to do!

I think that home cooks will appreciate Tina's skill in translating her years in the professional pastry world to creating simple recipes that will always work in the home kitchen. How marvelous to have all of the base recipes to perfect and then add so many appealing variations to the mix. I'm so happy that Milk & Cookies Bakery is a neighbor and I can pop in anytime I need my "cookie fix." And for those of you who don't live close by, Tina has given you a wonderfully enticing batch of recipes from which to bake your own.

*Jacques Torres*

INTROD

UCTION

# MILK AND COOKIES:

## THESE WORDS EMBRACE US WITH

## SWEET FLAVOR, SUGARY AROMA, AND COZY

## CHILDHOOD MEMORIES.

## THESE WORDS ARE PART OF MY DNA.

One of my first memories is of a kitchen table surrounded by women. Their loving, capable hands shaped, rolled, sugared, and cut cookie dough. As a tiny child, I wasn't even as tall as the table but I wanted to be part of this ritual. I knew they were preparing for a wedding, holiday, or family gathering. These women came together to bake cookies for a celebration.

At first I simply watched as they wrapped almond paste in little pockets of dough. So quick! So neat! Nimble fingers shaped tiny bows of dough, then placed one on each cookie. As I grew bigger, this became my job; my little fingers were the ideal size for twisting the dough into bows. This was my first kitchen task, and I was so proud to be part of the group. I tried to form each bow perfectly so the women I loved would be proud of me.

These ladies—my mother, grandmother, aunts, and great-aunts—all came together to bake. It usually started early Sunday afternoon, with a break for a huge pasta dinner. Even now, I close my eyes and feel the closeness and comfort of these women as they worked, chatting and laughing, and created perfect cookies that they shared with family, friends, and neighbors.

Some of these ladies became identified with one special cookie. There were Grandma Tina's Chocolate Drop Cookies (page 127), expertly iced drops of

heavenly chocolatey-ness with a wee walnut piece in the center. Aunt Annie's Sesame Seed Cookies (page 133) were perfectly rolled into logs and coated with sesame seeds.

Aunt Rose made her famous Viscotti or "S" Cookies (page 132). These cookies are a family heirloom, passed down from my great-grandmother to her daughters-in-law, Aunt Rose and Grandma Tina, so they could make them for their husbands exactly the same way she had. Also passed down was the requirement that they be baked fresh every day—the men only liked them on the same day they were baked!

Each of these cookies had its unique mark—a nuance in flavor or texture—that made it stand out on a tray of similar cookies baked by other women.

As soon as I could read and write, I made my own grocery lists and asked my father to take me shopping to buy cookie ingredients. I loved classic Italian cookies, but I also trolled my mother's food magazines for new recipes to introduce to the family. At Christmas, I gave everyone the same gift: a fancy package of my cookie creations.

I kept baking into my teen years without an inkling that cookies would be my future. I worked alongside my father in our pizza/sandwich/ice-cream shop in Rochester, New York. I loved working with food so much that I decided to take myself seriously and become a chef. I enrolled in the Culinary Institute of America, where so many of America's great chefs had trained. What I discovered about kitchen life can be summed up in one sentence: I was far more interested in making pastry than anything else!

After graduation, I moved to New York City to begin my pastry career. I worked in four-star restaurants, bakeries, and cafés; with caterers; at wholesale commissaries—anywhere to develop and hone my pastry skills. You name it, I baked it, but cookies were always my favorite.

In 1996, I heard about the perfect job: pastry instructor at the French Culinary institute. The pastry program at FCI was brand-new and had been developed by Jacques Torres, renowned pastry chef and chocolatier. I was chosen to become one of the first instructors. I thought, "Great, this is a temporary job while I plan my own business." Now, fifteen years later, I'm rich in experience and also the director of pastry and baking arts.

All of this was preparation for a full-time life in cookies. The Milk & Cookies chapter of my life began when a friend called to say that a little bakery in Greenwich Village was for sale. She told me, "You've got to buy it! It's your dream!" I didn't honestly think I had the ability to buy a business but curiosity got the better of me so I went to check out the place. After one minute inside the bakery, enveloped in the smell of freshly baked cookies, I knew; "This is right." I had to have it!

I carried that feeling with me, "This bakery will be mine." I would bring back my childhood passions for baking and eating freshly baked cookies with my family and friends. I would spend the day baking and serving cookies to enthralled customers. I would live for the simple love of milk and cookies every day.

Now, four years later, Milk & Cookies Bakery is my pride and joy. All day long, the sweet, honeyed aroma of freshly baking cookies fills the air. Not only do we bake cookies every day, we also throw in-store baking parties and create custom flavors for special orders. Working with a number of base recipes, each baker can choose any one he or she wants and, with additions, create a signature Milk & Cookies cookie.

I thought that cookie parties would be a child's dream and that most of my customers would be little ones celebrating birthdays and special occasions. But cookie making is everybody's favorite kitchen pastime. Young or old, women or men, rich or not so rich, all types, sizes, and colors of cookie lovers have sat at our big work tables creating their own style of cookies. It's so wonderful to watch the satisfaction my customers exude as they create their master-pieces. The life I lead is sugarcoated!

Since I believe all good things should be shared, in this book I give you all of my favorite cookie recipes so you can fill your kitchen with the same sweet moments I experience every day at Milk & Cookies Bakery. I hope you will be inspired to create your own variations on my favorites. And if you do, I hope that you, in turn, will share your favorites with me.

*Tina-Marie Cassacili*

# HOW TO

## CREATE

# NEVER-FAIL

# COOKIE

# DOUGH

The professional knowledge and skills I've gained through my years at the bakery have enabled me to create a wide variety of never-fail cookie doughs. I want to share three important bits of advice with you that I know will help give you a complete understanding of the techniques I use to create successful and delicious baked products.

My first bit of advice is to purchase a good-quality electronic scale; these are now quite inexpensive and are available from most kitchenware stores as well as many large supermarkets. One of the biggest mistakes home bakers make when preparing cookie dough is in the scaling (the professional term for measuring) of the ingredients. Concise measurement is probably the most important part of dough-making and it must be done meticulously. Weighing ingredients instead of using measuring cups (for both liquid and dry measurement) is absolutely the only accurate way to scale each ingredient.

My next bit of advice is for the mixing process. All bakers have a tendency to overmix doughs. As much as I love my electric mixer and could not live without it, it is a dangerous piece of equipment, for it can very quickly overmix almost any dough. To prevent this, I always finish mixing by hand and I suggest that you do this, too. Stop the mixer while the dough is still streaky and the ingredients are not fully blended together. Lightly flour a clean, flat work surface. Scrape the dough onto the surface, lightly flour your hands, and finish blending the dough using a gentle kneading motion, working until the dough is just combined. One warning: Keep in mind that there

are some doughs (usually with a high liquid content) such as Biscotti (page 114), Gingersnaps (page 91), or Snickerdoodles (page 87) that are supposed to be sticky, which gives the baked cookie a very specific texture.

Equal in importance to the first two bits of advice is the quality of the ingredients. If you want premium cookies, you need to start with premium ingredients. This means all the ingredients! We often purchase high-quality butter, flour, chocolate, and natural flavorings but take all of the lesser ingredients with a grain of salt. And speaking of salt, I always use sea salt and the finest-quality sweeteners I can purchase. Taking the time to find the perfect, premium ingredients will definitely pay off with perfect, top-quality baked goods.

If you incorporate these three very easy bits of advice into your dough preparation, I know you will find that you are making never-fail cookies every time you bake.

# CHAPTER 1

# VANILLA COOKIES

# Vanilla Base Dough

At Milk & Cookies, this is the dough we use most frequently. It is the base for our classic chocolate chip cookies as well as many other popular variations. The inclusion of finely ground oats or oat flour gives the dough a texture that is both crispy and chewy. Only the best pure vanilla extract is used because it gives a truer and deeper vanilla essence than any imitation flavor does. You can add just about anything you want to this dough and it will always be scrumptious! Or, you can bake it plain and still have a wonderful, simple, dunkingly delicious cookie.

**MAKES ABOUT 2 DOZEN COOKIES**

2½ cups (7½ ounces) old-fashioned rolled oats

2 cups (8 ounces) all-purpose flour

1 teaspoon baking powder

1 teaspoon baking soda

½ teaspoon salt

1½ cups (12 ounces) unsalted butter, at room temperature

1 cup (7 ounces) granulated sugar

1 cup (7 ounces) light brown sugar

2 large eggs, at room temperature

½ tablespoon pure vanilla extract

Preheat the oven to 350°F.

Line two baking sheets with nonstick silicone baking mats or parchment paper. (Alternatively, use nonstick baking sheets or lightly butter conventional baking sheets.) Set aside.

Put the oats in the bowl of a food processor fitted with the metal blade and process until finely ground. Transfer the ground oats to a mixing bowl. Stir in the flour, baking powder, baking soda, and salt. Set aside.

Put the butter in the bowl of a standing electric mixer fitted with the paddle. Begin beating on low speed to soften. Increase the speed to medium and beat for about 3 minutes, or until light and creamy.

With the motor running, gradually add the granulated sugar and then the brown sugar, beating until very light and creamy.

Add the eggs, one at a time, and beat to incorporate, scraping down the sides of the bowl with a rubber spatula after each addition. Beat in the vanilla and when blended, slowly beat in the reserved dry mixture.

While the dough is still streaky, remove the bowl from the mixer and scrape the paddle clean.

Lightly flour a clean, flat work surface.

Scrape the dough onto the floured surface. Lightly flour your hands and finish mixing the dough by using a gentle kneading motion, working until the dough is just blended. Do not overwork the dough, you want to be certain that all of the ingredients are blended together.

Using a tablespoon or small ice-cream scoop, make mounds of dough. Roll the dough into balls about $1\frac{1}{2}$ inches in diameter. Place the balls, about 2 inches apart, on the prepared baking sheets. Using your palm, gently flatten each ball to make a puck-like shape about 2 inches in diameter.

When all of the cookies are formed, place in the oven and bake for about 15 minutes, or until lightly browned around the edges and set in the center. Do not overbake; you want some chewiness in the center.

Remove from the oven and, using a metal spatula, transfer the cookies to wire racks to cool.

Store, airtight, at room temperature for up to a week.

**NOTE:** Dough can be stored, airtight, in the refrigerator for up to a week or in the freezer for up to a month.

# Milk & Cookies Bakery Classic Chocolate Chip Cookies

This is, by far, the biggest seller at Milk & Cookies Bakery. Each day, we make double the amount of chocolate chip to any other kind of cookie. We use chocolate curls that melt in the dough, creating threads of chocolate throughout. Having the chocolate curls in addition to the chocolate chunks ensures chocolate deliciousness in every bite.

**MAKES ABOUT 2 DOZEN COOKIES**

Vanilla Base Dough (page 20)

2 cups (12 ounces) semisweet chocolate chunks

2 cups (4 ounces) bittersweet chocolate curls or shavings

Preheat the oven to 350°F.

Line two baking sheets with nonstick silicone baking mats or parchment paper. (Alternatively, use nonstick baking sheets or lightly butter conventional baking sheets.) Set aside.

Prepare the Vanilla Base Dough. While the dough is still streaky, remove the bowl from the mixer and scrape the paddle clean.

Lightly flour a clean, flat work surface.

Scrape the dough onto the floured surface. Lightly flour your hands and finish mixing the dough by using a gentle kneading motion, working until the dough is just blended. Do not overwork the dough, you want to be certain that all of the ingredients are just blended together.

Using a wooden spoon, stir in the chocolate chunks and curls, mixing until evenly distributed. You can also do this in the mixer, but heavy mixing tends to break up the chocolate chunks and the baked cookies will have an undesirable dry texture.

Using a tablespoon or small ice-cream scoop, make mounds of dough. Roll the dough into balls about 1½ inches in diameter. Place the balls, about 2 inches apart, on the prepared baking sheets. Using your palm, gently flatten each ball to make a puck-like shape about 2 inches in diameter.

When all of the cookies are formed, place in the oven and bake for about 15 minutes, or until lightly browned around the edges and set in the center. Do not overbake; you want some chewiness in the center.

Remove from the oven and, using a metal spatula, transfer the cookies to wire racks to cool.

Store, airtight, at room temperature for up to a week.

# Milk Chocolate-Caramel Cookies

This is a cookie that thinks it is a candy bar. Milk chocolate and caramel mingle with moist, chewy cookie dough to make this one of our most-requested treats.

**MAKES ABOUT 2 DOZEN COOKIES**

Vanilla Base Dough (page 20)

2 cups (12 ounces) milk chocolate chips

2 cups (14 ounces) caramel bits (see Note)

Preheat the oven to 350ºF.

Line two baking sheets with nonstick silicone baking mats or parchment paper. (Alternatively, use nonstick baking sheets or lightly butter conventional baking sheets.) Set aside.

Prepare the Vanilla Base Dough. While the dough is still streaky, remove the bowl from the mixer and scrape the paddle clean.

Lightly flour a clean, flat work surface.

Scrape the dough onto the floured surface. Lightly flour your hands and finish mixing the dough by using a gentle kneading motion, working until the dough is just blended. Do not overwork the dough, you want to be certain that all of the ingredients are just blended together.

Using a wooden spoon, stir in the chocolate chips and caramel bits, mixing until evenly distributed. You can also do this in the mixer, but heavy mixing tends to break up the chocolate chips and caramel bits and the baked cookies will have an undesirable dry texture.

Using a tablespoon or small ice-cream scoop, make mounds of dough. Roll the dough into balls about 1½ inches in diameter. Place the balls, about 2 inches apart, on the prepared baking sheets. Using your palm, gently flatten each ball to make a puck-like shape about 2 inches in diameter.

When all of the cookies are formed, place in the oven and bake for about 15 minutes, or until lightly browned around the edges and set in the center. Do not overbake; you want some chewiness in the center.

Remove from the oven and, using a metal spatula, transfer the cookies to wire racks to cool.

Store, airtight, at room temperature for up to a week.

**NOTE:** If you can't find caramel bits, you can make them by cutting square caramel candies into small pieces.

# Milk Chocolate-Orange Cookies

The flavors in this cookie are quite subtle but very enticing. A hint of orange combined with the milk chocolate changes the base dough completely, giving it incomparable richness.

**MAKES ABOUT 2 DOZEN COOKIES**

Vanilla Base Dough (page 20)

2 tablespoons Grand Marnier liqueur

2 tablespoons freshly grated orange zest

2 cups (12 ounces) milk chocolate chunks

1 cup (4 ounces) coarsely chopped pecans

Preheat the oven to 350°F.

Line two baking sheets with nonstick silicone baking mats or parchment paper. (Alternatively, use nonstick baking sheets or lightly butter conventional baking sheets.) Set aside.

Prepare the Vanilla Base Dough. While the dough is still streaky, beat in the liqueur and orange zest. Remove the bowl from the mixer and scrape the paddle clean.

Lightly flour a clean, flat work surface.

Scrape the dough onto the floured surface. Lightly flour your hands and finish mixing the dough by using a gentle kneading motion, working until the dough is just blended. Do not overwork the dough, you want to be certain that all of the ingredients are just blended together.

Using a wooden spoon, stir in the chocolate and pecans, mixing until evenly distributed. You can also do this in the mixer, but heavy mixing tends to break up the chocolate and nuts and the baked cookies will have an undesirable dry texture.

Using a tablespoon or small ice-cream scoop, make mounds of dough. Roll the dough into balls about 1½ inches in diameter. Place the balls, about 2 inches apart, on the prepared baking sheets. Using your palm, gently flatten each ball to make a puck-like shape about 2 inches in diameter.

When all of the cookies are formed, place in the oven and bake for about 15 minutes, or until lightly browned around the edges and set in the center. Do not overbake; you want some chewiness in the center.

Remove from the oven and, using a metal spatula, transfer the cookies to wire racks to cool.

Store, airtight, at room temperature for up to a week.

# White Chocolate-Macadamia Nut Cookies

If you are a white chocolate lover, this is the cookie for you. I love this combination; white chocolate and macadamia nuts are perfect partners—rich and sweet.

**MAKES ABOUT 2 DOZEN COOKIES**

Vanilla Base Dough (page 20)

**2 cups (12 ounces) white chocolate chips**

**2 cups (8 ounces) chopped macadamia nuts**

Preheat the oven to 350°F.

Line two baking sheets with nonstick silicone baking mats or parchment paper. (Alternatively, use nonstick baking sheets or lightly butter conventional baking sheets.) Set aside.

Prepare the Vanilla Base Dough. While the dough is still streaky, remove the bowl from the mixer and scrape the paddle clean.

Lightly flour a clean, flat work surface.

Scrape the dough onto the floured surface. Lightly flour your hands and finish mixing the dough by using a gentle kneading motion, working until the dough is just blended. Do not overwork the dough, you want to be certain that all of the ingredients are just blended together.

Using a wooden spoon, stir in the chocolate and macadamia nuts, mixing until evenly distributed. You can also do this in the mixer, but heavy mixing tends to break up the chocolate and nuts and the baked cookies will have an undesirable dry texture.

Using a tablespoon or small ice-cream scoop, make mounds of dough. Roll the dough into balls about 1½ inches in diameter. Place the balls, about 2 inches apart, on the prepared baking sheets. Using your palm, gently flatten each ball to make a puck-like shape about 2 inches in diameter.

When all of the cookies are formed, place in the oven and bake for about 15 minutes, or until lightly browned around the edges and set in the center. Do not overbake; you want some chewiness in the center.

Remove from the oven and, using a metal spatula, transfer the cookies to wire racks to cool.

Store, airtight, at room temperature for up to a week.

# White Chocolate-Cherry Cookies

In this cookie, the cherries add just enough tartness to balance the sweetness of the chocolate and vanilla dough. Be sure to start with nice plump cherries to ensure maximum chewiness and flavor.

**MAKES ABOUT 2 DOZEN COOKIES**

Vanilla Base Dough (page 20)

2 cups (12 ounces) white chocolate chips

1 cup (6 ounces) dried cherries

1 cup (4 ounces) chopped pecans

Preheat the oven to 350ºF.

Line two baking sheets with nonstick silicone baking mats or parchment paper. (Alternatively, use nonstick baking sheets or lightly butter conventional baking sheets.) Set aside.

Prepare the Vanilla Base Dough. While the dough is still streaky, remove the bowl from the mixer and scrape the paddle clean.

Lightly flour a clean, flat work surface.

Scrape the dough onto the floured surface. Lightly flour your hands and finish mixing the dough by using a gentle kneading motion, working until the dough is just blended. Do not overwork the dough, you want to be certain that all of the ingredients are just blended together.

Using a wooden spoon, stir in the chocolate, cherries, and pecans, mixing until evenly distributed. You can also do this in the mixer, but heavy mixing tends to break up the chocolate and pecans and mash the cherries, and the baked cookies will have an undesirable dry texture.

Using a tablespoon or small ice-cream scoop, make mounds of dough. Roll the dough into balls about $1\frac{1}{2}$ inches in diameter. Place the balls, about 2 inches apart, on the prepared baking sheets. Using your palm, gently flatten each ball to make a puck-like shape about 2 inches in diameter.

When all of the cookies are formed, place in the oven and bake for about 15 minutes, or until lightly browned around the edges and set in the center. Do not overbake; you want some chewiness in the center.

Remove from the oven and, using a metal spatula, transfer the cookies to wire racks to cool.

Store, airtight, at room temperature for up to a week.

# Dark Chocolate-Toffee Cookies

These are one of my favorite cookies. The bittersweet chocolate flavor and the crunchy caramel notes from the toffee make a great pairing. This is a mature version of a candy bar that is also one of my favorites!

**MAKES ABOUT 2 DOZEN COOKIES**

Vanilla Base Dough (page 20)

**2 cups (12 ounces) bittersweet chocolate chunks**

**2 cups (12 ounces) toffee bits (see Note)**

Preheat the oven to 350°F.

Line two baking sheets with nonstick silicone baking mats or parchment paper. (Alternatively, use nonstick baking sheets or lightly butter conventional baking sheets.) Set aside.

Prepare the Vanilla Base Dough. While the dough is still streaky, remove the bowl from the mixer and scrape the paddle clean.

Lightly flour a clean, flat work surface.

Scrape the dough onto the floured surface. Lightly flour your hands and finish mixing the dough by using a gentle kneading motion, working until the dough is just blended. Do not overwork the dough, you want to be certain that all of the ingredients are just blended together.

Using a wooden spoon, stir in the chocolate and toffee, mixing until evenly distributed. You can also do this in the mixer, but heavy mixing tends to break up the chocolate and toffee and the baked cookies will have an undesirable dry texture.

Using a tablespoon or small ice-cream scoop, make mounds of dough. Roll the dough into balls about 1½ inches in diameter. Place the balls, about 2 inches apart, on the prepared baking sheets. Using your palm, gently flatten each ball to make a puck-like shape about 2 inches in diameter.

When all of the cookies are formed, place in the oven and bake for about 15 minutes, or until lightly browned around the edges and set in the center. Do not overbake; you want some chewiness in the center.

Remove from the oven and, using a metal spatula, transfer the cookies to wire racks to cool.

Store, airtight, at room temperature for up to a week.

**NOTE:** If toffee bits are not available, chop any toffee-flavored candy bar into small bits.

# Walnut Cookies

It is an amazing transformation: the addition of walnuts and a touch of walnut liqueur to the vanilla base. The result is a deliciously buttery cookie with a haunting walnut flavor.

**MAKES ABOUT 2 DOZEN COOKIES**

**Vanilla Base Dough (page 20)**

**2 tablespoons Nocino or other walnut liqueur**

**3 cups (12 ounces) large walnut pieces**

Preheat the oven to 350°F.

Line two baking sheets with nonstick silicone baking mats or parchment paper. (Alternatively, use nonstick baking mats or lightly butter conventional baking sheets.) Set aside.

Prepare the Vanilla Base Dough. While the dough is still streaky, beat in the liqueur. Remove the bowl from the mixer and scrape the paddle clean.

Lightly flour a clean, flat work surface.

Scrape the dough onto the floured surface. Lightly flour your hands and finish mixing the dough by using a gentle kneading motion, working until the dough is just blended. Do not overwork the dough, you want to be certain that all of the ingredients are just blended together.

Using a wooden spoon, stir in the walnuts, mixing until evenly distributed. You can also do this in the mixer, but heavy mixing tends to break up the nuts and the baked cookies will have an undesirable dry texture.

Using a tablespoon or small ice-cream scoop, make mounds of dough. Roll the dough into balls about 1½ inches in diameter. Place the balls, about 2 inches apart, on the prepared baking sheets. Using your palm, gently flatten each ball to make a puck-like shape about 2 inches in diameter.

When all of the cookies are formed, place in the oven and bake for about 15 minutes, or until lightly browned around the edges and set in the center. Do not overbake; you want some chewiness in the center.

Remove from the oven and, using a metal spatula, transfer the cookies to wire racks to cool.

Store, airtight, at room temperature for up to a week.

# CHAPTER 2

# DOUBLE CHOCOLATE COOKIES

# Dark Chocolate Base Dough

This dough has a unique consistency, falling somewhere between a cookie and a cake in texture. At Milk & Cookies Bakery, we use it for a wide variety of moist, rich cookies. If you are a chocolate lover like me, this cookie base will satisfy even the most intensely decadent, midnight chocoholic's craving. Because of its richness, we use only the highest-quality dark cocoa powder and recommend that you do the same. If you want to take the finished cookies to the chocolate limit, ice them with the Chocolate Frosting (page 128). Heaven on Earth!

**MAKES ABOUT 2 DOZEN COOKIES**

$2\frac{1}{4}$ cups (10 ounces) all-purpose flour

$\frac{1}{4}$ cup ($\frac{3}{4}$ ounce) Dutch-processed cocoa powder

1 teaspoon baking soda

$\frac{1}{2}$ teaspoon salt

1 cup (8 ounces) unsalted butter, at room temperature

$\frac{3}{4}$ cup (5 ounces) granulated sugar

$\frac{3}{4}$ cup (5 ounces) light brown sugar

2 large eggs, at room temperature

1 tablespoon pure vanilla extract

$1\frac{1}{2}$ cups (9 ounces) semisweet chocolate chips

Preheat the oven to 350°F.

Line two baking sheets with nonstick silicone baking mats or parchment paper. (Alternatively, use nonstick baking sheets or lightly butter conventional baking sheets.) Set aside.

Combine the flour, cocoa powder, baking soda, and salt in a mixing bowl. Set aside.

Put the butter in the bowl of a standing electric mixer fitted with the paddle. Begin beating on low speed to soften. Increase the speed to medium and beat for about 3 minutes, or until light and creamy.

With the motor running, gradually add the granulated sugar and then the brown sugar, beating until very light and creamy.

Combine the eggs with the vanilla. Add the egg mixture in two parts and beat to incorporate, scraping down the sides of the bowl with a rubber spatula after each addition.

Gradually add the reserved dry ingredients, beating until just streaky.

Remove the bowl from the mixer and scrape the paddle clean.

Lightly flour a clean, flat work surface.

Scrape the dough onto the floured surface. Lightly flour your hands and finish mixing the dough by using a gentle kneading motion, working until the dough is just blended. Do not overwork the dough, you want to be certain that all of the ingredients are just blended together.

Using a wooden spoon, stir in the chocolate chips, mixing until evenly distributed. You can also do this in the mixer but heavy mixing tends to break up the chocolate and the baked cookies will have an undesirable dry texture.

Using a tablespoon or small ice-cream scoop, make mounds of dough. Roll the dough into balls about $1\frac{1}{2}$ inches in diameter. Place the balls, about 2 inches apart, on the prepared baking sheets. Using your palm, gently flatten the top of each cookie slightly.

When all of the cookies are formed, place in the oven and bake for about 15 minutes, or until lightly browned around the edges. The center should be slightly soft to the touch.

Remove from the oven and, using a metal spatula, transfer the cookies to wire racks to cool.

Store, airtight, at room temperature for up to a week.

**NOTE:** Dough can be stored, airtight, in the refrigerator for up to a week or in the freezer for up to a month.

# Double Chocolate Chip-Mint Cookies

Chocolate and mint is one of my favorite combinations. The slight spiciness of the mint and the richness of the chocolate create a balance of flavors. At the bakery, we use Guittard mint-flavored chips, but there a number of other ways to create mint flavor in this base: crushed hard peppermint candies, a dash of mint extract, or mint liqueur are a few interesting variations.

**MAKES ABOUT 2 DOZEN COOKIES**

**Dark Chocolate Base Dough (page 34), omitting the vanilla extract**

**1 teaspoon pure peppermint extract**

**1½ cups (9 ounces) mint-flavored chocolate chips**

Preheat the oven to 350°F.

Line two baking sheets with nonstick silicone baking mats or parchment paper. (Alternatively, use nonstick baking sheets or lightly butter conventional baking sheets.) Set aside.

Prepare the Dark Chocolate Base Dough, replacing the vanilla extract with the peppermint extract. While the dough is still streaky, remove the bowl from the mixer and scrape the paddle clean.

Lightly flour a clean, flat work surface.

Scrape the dough onto the floured surface. Lightly flour your hands and finish mixing the dough by using a gentle kneading motion, working until the dough is just blended. Do not overwork the dough, you want to be certain that all of the ingredients are just blended together.

Using a wooden spoon, stir in the mint-flavored chips when adding the base recipe's semisweet chocolate chips to the dough, mixing until evenly distributed. You can also do this in the mixer, but heavy mixing tends to break up the chips and the baked cookies will have an undesirable dry texture.

Using a tablespoon or small ice-cream scoop, make mounds of dough. Roll the dough into balls about 1½ inches in diameter. Place the balls, about 2 inches apart, on the prepared baking sheets. Using your palm, gently flatten the top of each cookie slightly.

When all of the cookies are formed, place in the oven and bake for about 15 minutes, or until lightly browned around the edges. The center should be slightly soft to the touch.

Remove from the oven and, using a metal spatula, transfer the cookies to wire racks to cool.

Store, airtight, at room temperature for up to a week.

# Mocha Latte Cookies

This cookie is very reminiscent of freshly brewed cappuccino. It has the same exquisite, full-bodied flavor.

**MAKES ABOUT 2 DOZEN COOKIES**

**Dark Chocolate Base Dough (page 34)**

**1 tablespoon pure coffee extract**

**1½ cups (9 ounces) milk chocolate chunks**

Preheat the oven to 350ºF.

Line two baking sheets with nonstick silicone baking mats or parchment paper. (Alternatively, use nonstick baking sheets or lightly butter conventional baking sheets.) Set aside.

Prepare the Dark Chocolate Base Dough, adding the coffee extract along with the vanilla. While the dough is still streaky, remove the bowl from the mixer and scrape the paddle clean.

Lightly flour a clean, flat work surface.

Scrape the dough onto the floured surface. Lightly flour your hands and finish mixing the dough by using a gentle kneading motion, working until the dough is just blended. Do not overwork the dough, you want to be certain that all of the ingredients are just blended together.

Using a wooden spoon, stir in the milk chocolate chunks when adding the base recipe's semisweet chocolate chips to the dough, mixing until evenly distributed. You can also do this in the mixer, but heavy mixing tends to break up the chunks and chips and the baked cookies will have an undesirable dry texture.

Using a tablespoon or small ice-cream scoop, make mounds of dough. Roll the dough into balls about 1½ inches in diameter. Place the balls, about 2 inches apart, on the prepared baking sheets. Using your palm, gently flatten the top of each cookie slightly.

When all of the cookies are formed, place in the oven and bake for about 15 minutes, or until lightly browned around the edges. The center should be slightly soft to the touch.

Remove from the oven and, using a metal spatula, transfer the cookies to wire racks to cool.

Store, airtight, at room temperature for up to a week.

# Chocolate-Peanut Butter Cookies

Who doesn't love, love, love peanut butter and chocolate? Fortunes have been made dressing up this combination. These cookies are a bakery favorite, both with the staff and with our customers.

**MAKES ABOUT 2 DOZEN COOKIES**

Dark Chocolate Base Dough (page 34)

$1\frac{1}{2}$ cups ($9\frac{1}{2}$ ounces) peanut butter chips

1 cup (8 ounces) smooth peanut butter

Preheat the oven to 350°F.

Line two baking sheets with nonstick silicone baking mats or parchment paper. (Alternatively, use nonstick baking sheets or lightly butter conventional baking sheets.) Set aside.

Prepare the Dark Chocolate Base Dough. While the dough is still streaky, remove the bowl from the mixer and scrape the paddle clean.

Lightly flour a clean, flat work surface.

Scrape the dough onto the floured surface. Lightly flour your hands and finish mixing the dough by using a gentle kneading motion, working until the dough is just blended. Do not overwork the dough, you want to be certain that all of the ingredients are just blended together.

Using a wooden spoon, stir in the peanut butter chips and peanut butter when adding the base recipe's semisweet chocolate chips to the dough, leaving the peanut butter in heavy streaks or chunks throughout the dough.

Using a tablespoon, place mounds of the dough, about 2 inches apart, on the prepared baking sheets. Place in the oven and bake for about 20 minutes, or until lightly browned around the edges. The center should be slightly soft to the touch.

Remove from the oven and, using a metal spatula, transfer the cookies to wire racks to cool.

Store, airtight, at room temperature for up to a week.

# Chocolate-Almond Cookies

There's almost no better nut than almonds to use with chocolate. The tiny hint of bittersweet marries so well with the richness of the chocolate dough. Plus this cookie reminds me of one of my special treats—chocolate-covered almonds.

**MAKES ABOUT 2 DOZEN COOKIES**

Dark Chocolate Base Dough (page 34)

1 tablespoon almond extract

2 cups (8 ounces) toasted, coarsely chopped almonds

Preheat the oven to 350°F.

Line two baking sheets with nonstick silicone baking mats or parchment paper. (Alternatively, use nonstick baking sheets or lightly butter conventional baking sheets ) Set aside.

Prepare the Dark Chocolate Base Dough, adding the almond extract along with the vanilla. While the dough is still streaky remove the bowl from the mixer and scrape the paddle clean.

Lightly flour a clean, flat work surface.

Scrape the dough onto the floured surface. Lightly flour your hands and finish mixing the dough by using a gentle kneading motion, working until the dough is just blended. Do not overwork the dough, you want to be certain that all of the ingredients are just blended together.

Using a wooden spoon, stir in the almonds when adding the base recipe's semisweet chocolate chips to the dough, mixing until evenly distributed. You can also do this in the mixer, but heavy mixing tends to break up the chips and almonds and the baked cookies will have an undesirable dry texture.

Using a tablespoon or small ice-cream scoop, make mounds of dough. Roll the dough into balls about 1½ inches in diameter. Place the balls, about 2 inches apart, on the prepared baking sheets. Using your palm, gently flatten the top of each cookie slightly.

When all of the cookies are formed, place in the oven and bake for about 15 minutes, or until lightly browned around the edges. The center should be slightly soft to the touch.

Remove from the oven and, using a metal spatula, transfer the cookies to wire racks to cool.

Store, airtight, at room temperature for up to a week.

# Chocolate-Hazelnut Cookies

This cookie is rather like eating panini filled with Nutella, with the toasted hazelnuts adding that extra crunch.

**MAKES ABOUT 2 DOZEN COOKIES**

**Dark Chocolate Base Dough (page 34)**

**2 tablespoons Frangelico or other hazelnut liqueur**

**2 cups (8 ounces) toasted, coarsely chopped hazelnuts**

Preheat the oven to 350°F.

Line two baking sheets with nonstick silicone baking mats or parchment paper. (Alternatively, use nonstick baking sheets or lightly butter conventional baking sheets.) Set aside.

Prepare the Dark Chocolate Base Dough, adding the liqueur along with the vanilla. While the dough is still streaky, remove the bowl from the mixer and scrape the paddle clean.

Lightly flour a clean, flat work surface.

Scrape the dough onto the floured surface. Lightly flour your hands and finish mixing the dough by using a gentle kneading motion, working until the dough is just blended. Do not overwork the dough, you want to be certain that all of the ingredients are just blended together.

Using a wooden spoon, stir in the hazelnuts when adding the base recipe's semisweet chocolate chips to the dough, mixing until evenly distributed. You can also do this in the mixer, but heavy mixing tends to break up the chips and hazelnuts and the baked cookies will have an undesirable dry texture.

Using a tablespoon or small ice-cream scoop, make mounds of dough. Roll the dough into balls about 1½ inches in diameter. Place the balls, about 2 inches apart, on the prepared baking sheets. Using your palm, gently flatten the top of each cookie slightly.

When all of the cookies are formed, place in the oven and bake for about 15 minutes, or until lightly browned around the edges. The center should be slightly soft to the touch.

Remove from the oven and, using a metal spatula, transfer the cookies to wire racks to cool.

Store, airtight, at room temperature for up to a week.

# Candied Orange and Pistachio Cookies

This is the cookie version of one of my favorite childhood biscotti. Like biscotti, it's a perfect dunking cookie, particularly into a wonderful cup of orange spice tea or an espresso.

**MAKES ABOUT 2 DOZEN COOKIES**

Dark Chocolate Base Dough (page 34)

2 tablespoons Grand Marnier liqueur

2 cups (12 ounces) bittersweet chocolate chunks

1 cup (4 ounces) pistachios

3 tablespoons candied orange peel

Preheat the oven to 350°F.

Line two baking sheets with nonstick silicone baking mats or parchment paper. (Alternatively, use nonstick baking sheets or lightly butter conventional baking sheets.) Set aside.

Prepare the Dark Chocolate Base Dough. While the dough is still streaky, beat in the liqueur. Remove the bowl from the mixer and scrape the paddle clean.

Lightly flour a clean, flat work surface.

Scrape the dough onto the floured surface. Lightly flour your hands and finish mixing the dough by using a gentle kneading motion, working until the dough is just blended. Do not overwork the dough, you want to be certain that all of the ingredients are just blended together.

Using a wooden spoon, stir in the bittersweet chocolate chunks, pistachios, and candied orange peel when adding the base recipe's semisweet chocolate chips to the dough, mixing until evenly distributed. You can also do this in the mixer, but heavy mixing tends to break up the chips, chunks, and nuts and the baked cookies will have an undesirable dry texture.

Using a tablespoon or small ice-cream scoop, make mounds of dough. Roll the dough into balls about $1\frac{1}{2}$ inches in diameter. Place the balls, about 2 inches apart, on the prepared baking sheets. Using your palm, gently flatten the top of each cookie slightly.

When all of the cookies are formed, place in the oven and bake for about 15 minutes, or until lightly browned around the edges. The center should be slightly soft to the touch.

Remove from the oven and, using a metal spatula, transfer the cookies to wire racks to cool.

Store, airtight, at room temperature for up to a week.

# CHAPTER 3

# OATMEAL COOKIES

# Oatmeal Base Dough

There is nothing more classic than cookies made with this oatmeal cookie dough. They come out both chewy and crunchy. The hint of cinnamon makes them a bakery favorite. Our customers particularly enjoy them with a cup of steaming hot chocolate on a snowy Greenwich Village day.

**MAKES ABOUT 2 DOZEN COOKIES**

1½ cups (6 ounces) all-purpose flour

1 tablespoon ground cinnamon

1 teaspoon baking soda

½ teaspoon salt

1½ cups (12 ounces) unsalted butter, at room temperature

1 cup (7 ounces) light brown sugar, firmly packed

½ cup (3½ ounces) granulated sugar

2 large eggs, at room temperature

1 tablespoon pure vanilla extract

3 cups (9 ounces) old-fashioned rolled oats

Preheat the oven to 350°F.

Line two baking sheets with nonstick silicone baking mats or parchment paper. (Alternatively, use nonstick baking sheets or lightly butter conventional baking sheets.) Set aside.

Combine the flour, cinnamon, baking soda, and salt in a mixing bowl. Set aside.

Put the butter in the bowl of a standing electric mixer fitted with the paddle. Begin beating on low speed. Add the brown sugar and granulated sugar, increase the speed to medium, and beat for about 4 minutes, or until light and creamy.

Add the eggs, one at a time, and beat to incorporate, scraping down the sides of the bowl with a rubber spatula after each addition. Beat in the vanilla and when blended, slowly beat in the reserved dry mixture together with the oats.

While the dough is still streaky, remove the bowl from the mixer and scrape the paddle clean. It is very important not to overmix this dough or the cookies will be dry and hard when baked.

Lightly flour a clean, flat work surface.

Scrape the dough onto the floured surface. Lightly flour your hands and finish mixing the dough by using a gentle kneading motion, working until the dough is just blended. Do not overwork the dough, you want to be certain that all of the ingredients are just blended together.

Using a tablespoon or small ice-cream scoop, make mounds of dough. Roll the dough into balls about $1\frac{1}{2}$ inches in diameter. Place the balls, about 2 inches apart, on the prepared baking sheets. Using your palm, gently flatten the top of each cookie slightly.

When all of the cookies are formed, place in the oven and bake for about 15 minutes, or until lightly browned around the edges. The center should be slightly soft to the touch.

Remove from the oven and, using a metal spatula, transfer the cookies to wire racks to cool.

Store, airtight, at room temperature for up to a week.

**NOTE:** Dough can be stored, airtight, in the refrigerator for up to a week or in the freezer for up to a month.

# Scotchies

For a sweeter version of an oatmeal cookie, Scotchies do the trick. I love them warm, the butterscotch melting between the oats—a sensational taste treat!

**MAKES ABOUT 2 DOZEN COOKIES**

Oatmeal Base Dough (page 46)

2 cups (12 ounces) butterscotch chips

Preheat the oven to 350°F.

Line two baking sheets with nonstick silicone baking mats or parchment paper. (Alternatively, use nonstick baking sheets or lightly butter conventional baking sheets.) Set aside.

Prepare the Oatmeal Base Dough. While the dough is still streaky, remove the bowl from the mixer and scrape the paddle clean. It is very important not to overmix this dough or the cookies will be dry and hard when baked.

Lightly flour a clean, flat work surface.

Scrape the dough onto the floured surface. Lightly flour your hands and finish mixing the dough by using a gentle kneading motion, working until the dough is just blended. Do not overwork the dough, you want to be certain that all of the ingredients are just blended together.

Using a wooden spoon, stir in the butterscotch chips, mixing until evenly distributed. You can also do this in the mixer, but heavy mixing tends to break up the chips and the baked cookies will have an undesirable dry texture.

Using a tablespoon or small ice-cream scoop, make mounds of dough. Roll the dough into balls about 1½ inches in diameter. Place the balls, about 2 inches apart, on the prepared baking sheets. Using your palm, gently flatten the top of each cookie slightly.

When all of the cookies are formed, place in the oven and bake for about 15 minutes, or until lightly browned around the edges. The center should be slightly soft to the touch.

Remove from the oven and, using a metal spatula, transfer the cookies to wire racks to cool.

Store, airtight, at room temperature for up to a week.

# Spiced Oatmeal Cookies

This happens to be my favorite combination of spices, but feel free to make any combination that pleases your palate. You can even add a little heat if you like—not too much; even a hint of pure hot chile powder goes a long, long way!

**MAKES ABOUT 2 DOZEN COOKIES**

Oatmeal Base Dough (page 46)

2 teaspoons ground ginger

1 teaspoon ground cloves

1 teaspoon ground nutmeg

1 teaspoon ground cardamom

$\frac{1}{2}$ cup (3$\frac{1}{2}$ ounces) granulated sugar

$\frac{1}{2}$ tablespoon ground cinnamon

Preheat the oven to 350°F.

Line two baking sheets with nonstick silicone baking mats or parchment paper. (Alternatively, use nonstick baking sheets or lightly butter conventional baking sheets.) Set aside.

Prepare the Oatmeal Base Dough, adding the ginger, cloves, nutmeg, and cardamom along with the base recipe's dry ingredients. While the dough is still streaky, remove the bowl from the mixer and scrape the paddle clean.

Lightly flour a clean, flat work surface.

Combine the sugar and cinnamon on a small flat plate.

Scrape the dough onto the floured surface. Lightly flour your hands and finish mixing the dough by using a gentle kneading motion, working until the dough is just blended. Do not overwork the dough, you want to be certain that all of the ingredients are just blended together.

Using a tablespoon or small ice-cream scoop, make mounds of dough. Roll the dough into balls about 1$\frac{1}{2}$ inches in diameter. Working with one at a time, roll the balls in the cinnamon-sugar.

Place the balls, about 2 inches apart, on the baking sheets. Using your palm, gently flatten the top of each cookie slightly.

When all of the cookies are formed, place in the oven and bake for about 15 minutes, or until lightly browned around the edges. The center should be slightly soft to the touch.

Store, airtight, at room temperature for up to a week.

# Oatmeal-Raisin Cookies

There are many types of oatmeal cookies, but my favorite is an oatmeal-raisin that is soft and a bit chewy. This recipe delivers that, plus it is very moist and delicious! I sometimes use golden raisins to give a different spin or, from time to time, I use a mixture of golden and black.

**MAKES ABOUT 2 DOZEN COOKIES**

Oatmeal Base Dough (page 46)

1½ cups (9 ounces) raisins

Preheat the oven to 350°F.

Line two baking sheets with nonstick silicone baking mats or parchment paper. (Alternatively, use nonstick baking sheets or lightly butter conventional baking sheets.) Set aside.

Prepare the Oatmeal Base Dough. While the dough is still streaky, remove the bowl from the mixer and scrape the paddle clean. It is very important not to overmix this dough or the cookies will be dry and hard when baked.

Lightly flour a clean, flat work surface.

Scrape the dough onto the floured surface. Lightly flour your hands and finish mixing the dough by using a gentle kneading motion, working until the dough is just blended. Do not overwork the dough, you want to be certain that all of the ingredients are just blended together.

Using a wooden spoon, stir in the raisins, mixing until evenly distributed. You can also do this in the mixer, but heavy mixing tends to break up the raisins and the baked cookies will have an undesirable dry texture.

Using a tablespoon or small ice-cream scoop, make mounds of dough. Roll the dough into balls about 1½ inches in diameter. Place the balls, about 2 inches apart, on the prepared baking sheets. Using your palm, gently flatten the top of each cookie slightly.

When all of the cookies are formed, place in the oven and bake for about 15 minutes, or until lightly browned around the edges. The center should be slightly soft to the touch.

Remove from the oven and, using a metal spatula, transfer the cookies to wire racks to cool.

Store, airtight, at room temperature for up to a week.

# Blueberry-Oatmeal Cookies

My favorite winter breakfast is a bowl of warm, toasty oatmeal with blueberries stirred in at the last moment and a drizzle of warm maple syrup to finish. These cookies are a sweeter version of a healthful winter breakfast.

**MAKES ABOUT 2 DOZEN COOKIES**

Oatmeal Base Dough (page 46)

2 tablespoons pure maple syrup

2 cups (12 ounces) dried blueberries

Preheat the oven to 350°F.

Line two baking sheets with nonstick silicone baking mats or parchment paper. (Alternatively, use nonstick baking sheets or lightly butter conventional baking sheets.) Set aside.

Prepare the Oatmeal Base Dough, adding the maple syrup after all of the sugar has been incorporated. While the dough is still streaky, remove the bowl from the mixer and scrape the paddle clean.

Lightly flour a clean, flat work surface.

Scrape the dough onto the floured surface. Lightly flour your hands and finish mixing the dough by using a gentle kneading motion, working until the dough is just blended. Do not overwork the dough, you want to be certain that all of the ingredients are just blended together.

Using a wooden spoon, stir in the blueberries, mixing until evenly distributed. You can also do this in the mixer, but heavy mixing tends to break up the berries and the baked cookies will have an undesirable dry texture.

Using a tablespoon or small ice-cream scoop, make mounds of dough. Roll the dough into balls about 1 1/2 inches in diameter. Place the balls, about 2 inches apart, on the prepared baking sheets. Using your palm, gently flatten the top of each cookie slightly.

When all of the cookies are formed, place in the oven and bake for about 15 minutes, or until lightly browned around the edges. The center should be slightly soft to the touch.

Store, airtight, at room temperature for up to a week.

# Cranberry-Walnut Oatmeal Cookies

This comes from yet another favorite winter breakfast—a steaming bowl of hot oatmeal with tart-sweet cranberries and toasted walnut pieces mixed in. A great way to start the day and an even better (very-nearly) healthful afternoon snack.

**MAKES ABOUT 2 DOZEN COOKIES**

Oatmeal Base Dough (page 46)

$1\frac{1}{2}$ cups (9 ounces) dried cranberries

1 cup (4 ounces) chopped walnuts

Preheat the oven to 350°F.

Line two baking sheets with nonstick silicone baking mats or parchment paper. (Alternatively, use nonstick baking sheets or lightly butter conventional baking sheets.) Set aside.

Prepare the Oatmeal Base Dough. While the dough is still streaky, remove the bowl from the mixer and scrape the paddle clean. It is very important not to over mix this dough or the cookies will be dry and hard when baked.

Lightly flour a clean, flat work surface.

Scrape the dough onto the floured surface. Lightly flour your hands and finish mixing the dough by using a gentle kneading motion, working until the dough is just blended. Do not overwork the dough, you want to be certain that all of the ingredients are just blended together.

Using a wooden spoon, stir in the cranberries and walnuts, mixing until evenly distributed. You can also do this in the mixer, but heavy mixing tends to break up the cranberries and nuts and the baked cookies will have an undesirable dry texture.

Using a tablespoon or small ice-cream scoop, make mounds of dough. Roll the dough into balls about $1\frac{1}{2}$ inches in diameter. Place the balls, about 2 inches apart, on the prepared baking sheets. Using your palm, gently flatten the top of each cookie slightly.

When all of the cookies are formed, place in the oven and bake for about 15 minutes, or until lightly browned around the edges. The center should be slightly soft to the touch.

Remove from the oven and, using a metal spatula, transfer the cookies to wire racks to cool.

Store, airtight, at room temperature for up to a week.

# White Chocolate-Cherry Oatmeal Cookies

These cookies are always a late spring special at Milk & Cookies Bakery. The combination of tart cherries and white chocolate makes me think of the cherry trees that blossom along many Greenwich Village streets in the spring.

**MAKES ABOUT 2 DOZEN COOKIES**

2 cups (12 ounces) dried cherries

1 cup (8 ounces) fresh orange juice

Oatmeal Base Dough (page 46)

$1\frac{1}{2}$ cups (9 ounces) white chocolate chips

Put the cherries in a small heatproof container.

Put the orange juice in a small, nonreactive saucepan over medium heat and bring to a boil. Immediately remove from the heat and pour over the cherries. Set aside to plump for 30 minutes.

Drain the cherries through a fine-mesh sieve, discarding any excess liquid. Set the cherries aside.

Preheat the oven to 350ºF.

Line two baking sheets with nonstick silicone baking mats or parchment paper. (Alternatively, use nonstick baking sheets or lightly butter conventional baking sheets.) Set aside.

Prepare the Oatmeal Base Dough. While the dough is still streaky, remove the bowl from the mixer and scrape the paddle clean.

Lightly flour a clean, flat work surface.

Scrape the dough onto the floured surface. Lightly flour your hands and finish mixing the dough by using a gentle kneading motion, working until the dough is just blended. Do not overwork the dough, you want to be certain that all of the ingredients are just blended together.

Using a wooden spoon, stir in the chocolate chips and drained cherries, mixing until evenly distributed. You can also do this in the mixer, but heavy mixing tends to break up the chips and cherries and the baked cookies will have an undesirable dry texture.

Using a tablespoon or small ice-cream scoop, make mounds of dough. Roll the dough into balls about $1\frac{1}{2}$ inches in diameter. Place the balls, about 2 inches apart, on the prepared baking sheets. Using your palm, gently flatten the top of each cookie slightly.

When all of the cookies are formed, place in the oven and bake for about 15 minutes, or until lightly browned around the edges. The center should be slightly soft to the touch.

Remove from the oven and, using a metal spatula, transfer the cookies to wire racks to cool.

Store, airtight, at room temperature for up to a week.

# Milk Chocolate-Orange Oatmeal Cookies

The crunchy texture of oats makes the perfect base for milk chocolate and tangy orange zest. The touch of liqueur brings it all together, creating a marvelous sweetness.

**MAKES ABOUT 2 DOZEN COOKIES**

Oatmeal Base Dough (page 46)

2 tablespoons Grand Marnier liqueur

2 tablespoons freshly grated orange zest

2 cups (12 ounces) milk chocolate chunks

1 cup (4 ounces) chopped walnuts

Preheat the oven to 350°F.

Line two baking sheets with nonstick silicone baking mats or parchment paper. (Alternatively, use nonstick baking sheets or lightly butter conventional baking sheets.) Set aside.

Prepare the Oatmeal Base Dough, adding the liqueur and orange zest along with the vanilla. While the dough is still streaky, remove the bowl from the mixer and scrape the paddle clean.

Lightly flour a clean, flat work surface.

Scrape the dough onto the floured surface. Lightly flour your hands and finish mixing the dough by using a gentle kneading motion, working until the dough is just blended. Do not overwork the dough, you want to be certain that all of the ingredients are just blended together.

Using a wooden spoon, stir in the chocolate and walnuts, mixing until evenly distributed. You can also do this in the mixer, but heavy mixing tends to break up the chunks and nuts and the baked cookies will have an undesirable dry texture.

Using a tablespoon or small ice-cream scoop, make mounds of dough. Roll the dough into balls about $1\frac{1}{2}$ inches in diameter. Place the balls, about 2 inches apart, on the prepared baking sheets. Using your palm, gently flatten the top of each cookie slightly.

When all of the cookies are formed, place in the oven and bake for about 15 minutes, or until lightly browned around the edges. The center should be slightly soft to the touch.

Remove from the oven and, using a metal spatula, transfer the cookies to wire racks to cool.

Store, airtight, at room temperature for up to a week.

# Chocolate Chunk– Oatmeal Cookies

It's like combining two favorites to make one great cookie. The subtle cinnamon flavor goes well with the dark chocolate, and the oatmeal gives it a texture unlike regular chocolate chip cookies.

**MAKES ABOUT 2 DOZEN COOKIES**

Oatmeal Base Dough (page 46)

2 cups (12 ounces) semisweet chocolate chunks

Preheat the oven to 350°F.

Line two baking sheets with nonstick silicone baking mats or parchment paper. (Alternatively, use nonstick baking sheets or lightly butter conventional baking sheets.) Set aside.

Prepare the Oatmeal Base Dough. While the dough is still streaky, remove the bowl from the mixer and scrape the paddle clean. It is very important not to overmix this dough or the cookies will be dry and hard when baked.

Lightly flour a clean, flat work surface.

Scrape the dough onto the floured surface. Lightly flour your hands and finish mixing the dough by using a gentle kneading motion, working until the dough is just blended. Do not overwork the dough, you want to be certain that all of the ingredients are just blended together.

Using a wooden spoon, stir in the chocolate, mixing until evenly distributed. You can also do this in the mixer, but heavy mixing tends to break up the chunks and the baked cookies will have an undesirable dry texture.

Using a tablespoon or small ice-cream scoop, make mounds of dough. Roll the dough into balls about 1½ inches in diameter. Place the balls, about 2 inches apart, on the prepared baking sheets. Using your palm, gently flatten the top of each cookie slightly.

When all of the cookies are formed, place in the oven and bake for about 15 minutes, or until lightly browned around the edges. The center should be slightly soft to the touch.

Remove from the oven and, using a metal spatula, transfer the cookies to wire racks to cool.

Store, airtight, at room temperature for up to a week.

# CHAPTER 4

# PEANUT BUTTER COOKIES

# Peanut Butter Base Dough

Peanut butter cookies were my favorite teenage project because I thought the raw dough was as delicious as the cookies and I could snack on it during the making and the baking! I also loved scoring the cookies with a fork, making sure that each was marked perfectly.

The Milk & Cookies Bakery recipe is peanut butter perfection. The cookies are not so dry that they crumble when you pick them up nor so moist that they stick to the roof of your mouth, like their main ingredient. We use natural-style peanut butter without added sugar so the cookies have a true peanut taste. After much experimentation, we now have the flawless combination of texture and flavor.

**MAKES ABOUT 2 DOZEN COOKIES**

$1\frac{1}{2}$ cups (6 ounces) all-purpose flour

$\frac{1}{2}$ teaspoon baking soda

$\frac{1}{2}$ teaspoon baking powder

$\frac{1}{4}$ teaspoon salt

$1\frac{1}{2}$ cups (12 ounces) unsalted butter, at room temperature

1 cup (7 ounces) light brown sugar, firmly packed

1 cup (8 ounces) smooth peanut butter

2 large eggs, at room temperature

1 teaspoon pure vanilla extract

Combine the flour, baking soda, baking powder, and salt in a mixing bowl. Set aside.

Put the butter in the bowl of a standing electric mixer fitted with the paddle. Begin beating on low speed. Add the brown sugar, increase the speed to medium, and beat for about 4 minutes, or until light and creamy. Add the peanut butter and beat to incorporate; then, beat in the eggs, one at a time, scraping down the sides of the bowl with a rubber spatula after each addition. Beat in the vanilla.

With the motor running, gradually add the flour mixture, beating just to blend. While the dough is still streaky, remove the bowl from the mixer and scrape the paddle clean.

Lightly flour a clean, flat work surface.

Scrape the dough onto the floured surface. Lightly flour your hands and finish mixing the dough by using a gentle kneading motion, working until the dough is just blended. Do not overwork the dough, you want to be certain that all of the ingredients are just blended together.

Cover the dough tightly in plastic wrap. Refrigerate for at least 1 hour, or until firm.

When ready to bake, preheat the oven to 325°F.

Line two baking sheets with nonstick silicone baking mats or parchment paper. (Alternatively, use nonstick baking sheets or lightly butter conventional baking sheets.) Set aside.

Remove the dough from the refrigerator and unwrap.

Using a tablespoon or small ice-cream scoop, make mounds of dough. Roll the dough into balls about $1\frac{1}{2}$ inches in diameter. Place the balls, about 2 inches apart, on the prepared baking sheets. Using your palm, gently flatten the top of each cookie slightly. If you wish to create the traditional crisscross pattern on top of the cookies, press the surface using the tines of a fork.

When all of the cookies are formed, place in the oven and bake for about 8 minutes, or until golden brown around the edges.

Remove from the oven and, using a metal spatula, transfer the cookies to wire racks to cool.

Store, airtight, at room temperature for up to a week.

**NOTE:** Dough can be stored, airtight, in the refrigerator for up to a week or in the freezer for up to a month.

# Peanut Butter- Milk Chocolate Bites

Here is my take on the most famous peanut butter/chocolate candy of them all. It is a constant best-seller in the bakery, as well as one of the staff's favorites.

**MAKES ABOUT 2 DOZEN COOKIES**

Peanut Butter Base Dough (page 60)

2 cups (12 ounces) peanut butter chips

1 cup (4 ounces) coarsely chopped roasted, salted peanuts

1 cup (6 ounces) milk chocolate chunks or pistoles (see Note)

Prepare the Peanut Butter Base Dough, adding the peanut butter chips along with the dry ingredients, and mix to just barely blend. While the dough is still streaky, remove the bowl from the mixer and scrape the paddle clean.

Lightly flour a clean, flat work surface.

Scrape the dough onto the floured surface. Lightly flour your hands and finish mixing the dough by using a gentle kneading motion, working until the dough is just blended. Do not overwork the dough, you want to be certain that all of the ingredients are just blended together.

Cover the dough tightly in plastic wrap. Refrigerate for at least 1 hour, or until firm.

When ready to bake, preheat the oven to 325°F.

Line two baking sheets with nonstick silicone baking mats or parchment paper. (Alternatively, use nonstick baking sheets or lightly butter conventional baking sheets.) Set aside.

Place the peanuts on a large flat plate.

Remove the dough from the refrigerator and unwrap.

Using a tablespoon or small ice-cream scoop, make mounds of dough. Roll the dough into balls about 1½ inches in diameter. Working with one at a time, roll each ball in the peanuts to lightly coat.

Place the balls, about 2 inches apart, on the prepared baking sheets. Using your palm, gently flatten the top of each cookie. Using your thumb, make an indentation in the center. Place a chocolate chunk (or a few pistoles) in the indentation.

When all of the cookies are formed, place in the oven and bake for about 8 minutes, or until golden brown around the edges.

Remove from the oven and, using a metal spatula, transfer the cookies to wire racks to cool.

Store, airtight, at room temperature for up to a week.

**NOTE:** Chocolate pistoles are small, flat, chocolate disks used by professional bakers and candy makers. They are available at most specialty food shops and cake and bakery supply stores, and on the Internet.

# Crispy Peanut Butter Cookies

Rather than the soft, kinda-chewy traditional peanut butter cookie, these cookies are snappy and crisp. I love them with a cup of hot chocolate to get that classic chocolate/peanut butter combination going.

**MAKES ABOUT 2 DOZEN COOKIES**

Peanut Butter Base Dough (page 60)

**2 cups (8 ounces) finely chopped roasted, salted peanuts**

Prepare the Peanut Butter Base Dough, adding the peanuts along with the dry ingredients, and mix to just barely blend. While the dough is still streaky, remove the bowl from the mixer and scrape the paddle clean.

Lightly flour a clean, flat work surface.

Scrape the dough onto the floured surface. Lightly flour your hands and finish mixing the dough by using a gentle kneading motion, working until the dough is just blended. Do not overwork the dough, you want to be certain that all of the ingredients are just blended together.

Cover the dough tightly in plastic wrap. Refrigerate for at least 1 hour, or until firm.

When ready to bake, preheat the oven to 325°F.

Line two baking sheets with nonstick silicone baking mats or parchment paper. (Alternatively, use nonstick baking sheets or lightly butter conventional baking sheets.) Set aside.

Remove the dough from the refrigerator and unwrap.

Using a tablespoon or small ice-cream scoop, make mounds of dough. Roll the dough into balls about $1\frac{1}{2}$ inches in diameter. Place the balls, about 2 inches apart, on the prepared baking sheets. Using your palm, gently flatten the top of each cookie so that the dough is about $\frac{1}{4}$ inch thick. If you wish to create the traditional crisscross pattern on top of the cookies, press the surface using the tines of a fork.

When all of the cookies are formed, place in the oven and bake for about 8 minutes, or until golden brown around the edges.

Remove from the oven and, using a metal spatula, transfer the cookies to wire racks to cool.

Store, airtight, at room temperature for up to a week.

# Peanut Butter and Jelly Cookies

Wouldn't you rather have a cookie than a sandwich? This sweet treat fits the bill, especially when dunked into a glass of ice-cold milk. The perfect snack!

**MAKES 1 DOZEN SANDWICH COOKIES**

**Peanut Butter Base Dough (page 60)**

**$\frac{1}{2}$ cup (6 ounces) jam of choice**

Prepare the Peanut Butter Base Dough. While the dough is still streaky, remove the bowl from the mixer and scrape the paddle clean.

Lightly flour a clean, flat work surface.

Scrape the dough onto the floured surface. Lightly flour your hands and finish mixing the dough by using a gentle kneading motion, working until the dough is just blended. Do not overwork the dough, you want to be certain that all of the ingredients are just blended together.

Cover the dough tightly in plastic wrap. Refrigerate for at least 1 hour, or until firm.

When ready to bake, preheat the oven to 325°F.

Line two baking sheets with nonstick silicone baking mats or parchment paper. (Alternatively, use nonstick baking sheets or lightly butter conventional baking sheets.) Set aside.

Lightly flour a clean, flat work surface.

Remove the dough from the refrigerator and unwrap.

Place the dough in the center of the floured surface. Using a rolling pin, roll the dough out to a piece about $\frac{1}{2}$ inch thick. Using a 2-inch round biscuit cutter, cut out the cookies. Place the cookies, about 2 inches apart, on the prepared baking sheets. If you wish to create the traditional crisscross pattern on top of the cookies, press the surface using the tines of a fork.

When all of the cookies are formed, place in the oven and bake for about 5 minutes, or until golden brown around the edges.

Remove from the oven and, using a metal spatula, transfer the cookies to wire racks to cool.

When completely cool, spread the jam on the flat side of a cookie. Top with a second cookie, flat-side down, and press together gently.

Store, airtight, at room temperature for up to a week.

# Dark Chocolate-Peanut Butter Cookies

This is my adult version of that beloved combination. Try using different varieties of dark chocolate. Each will add a different dynamic of flavor and sweetness to the baked cookies. I guarantee that no matter what type you use, the cookies will be a hit.

**MAKES ABOUT 2 DOZEN COOKIES**

**Peanut Butter Base Dough (page 60)**

**1 cup (6 ounces) peanut butter chips**

**1 cup (6 ounces) bittersweet chocolate chips**

**1 cup (4 ounces) finely ground roasted, salted peanuts**

Prepare the Peanut Butter Base Dough, adding the peanut butter chips, chocolate chips, and peanuts along with the dry ingredients, and mix to just barely blend. While the dough is still streaky, remove the bowl from the mixer and scrape the paddle clean.

Lightly flour a clean, flat work surface.

Scrape the dough onto the floured surface. Lightly flour your hands and finish mixing the dough by using a gentle kneading motion, working until the dough is just blended. Do not overwork the dough, you want to be certain that all of the ingredients are just blended together.

Cover the dough tightly in plastic wrap. Refrigerate for at least 1 hour, or until firm.

When ready to bake, preheat the oven to 325°F.

Line two baking sheets with nonstick silicone baking mats or parchment paper. (Alternatively, use nonstick baking sheets or lightly butter conventional baking sheets.) Set aside.

Remove the dough from the refrigerator and unwrap.

Using a tablespoon or small ice-cream scoop, make mounds of dough. Roll the dough into balls about $1\frac{1}{2}$ inches in diameter. Place the balls, about 2 inches apart, on the prepared baking sheets. Using your palm, gently flatten the top of each cookie slightly.

When all of the cookies are formed, place in the oven and bake for about 8 minutes, or until golden brown around the edges.

Remove from the oven and, using a metal spatula, transfer the cookies to wire racks to cool.

Store, airtight, at room temperature for up to a week.

# CHAPTER 5

# SUGAR COOKIES

# Sugar Cookie Base Dough

Sugar Cookie Base Dough is perhaps my most versatile dough, and these wonderful cookies remain a customer favorite even with just a sprinkling of sugar on top. The dough makes a great base for additions. Let your imagination soar. Children particularly like this base dough because they can stir in so many of their favorite candies. Unlike other bases in this book, this dough can be rolled out to make cut-out cookies. After they are baked, they're the perfect cookie to be iced and decorated. No wonder they're a holiday favorite.

**MAKES ABOUT 2 DOZEN COOKIES**

3 cups (12 ounces) all-purpose flour

$1/2$ teaspoon salt

$1/4$ teaspoon baking soda

$1/4$ teaspoon cream of tartar

$1^1/2$ cups (12 ounces) unsalted butter, at room temperature

$1^1/4$ cups ($8^3/4$ ounces) superfine sugar

2 large egg yolks, at room temperature

2 teaspoons pure vanilla extract

2 tablespoons milk

$1/2$ cup ($3^1/2$ ounces) granulated sugar

Combine the flour, salt, baking soda, and cream of tartar in a mixing bowl. Set aside.

Put the butter in the bowl of a standing electric mixer fitted with the paddle. Begin beating on low speed. Increase the speed to medium and beat for about 3 minutes, or until very light and smooth.

Add the superfine sugar, $1/4$ cup at a time. When all of the sugar has been added, beat for 2 minutes.

Add the egg yolks, one at a time, scraping down the sides of the bowl with a rubber spatula after each addition. Add the vanilla and continue to beat for 1 minute.

With the motor running, add half of the flour mixture, followed by the milk. When blended, add the remaining flour and beat to just barely blend. While the dough is still streaky, remove the bowl from the mixer and scrape the paddle clean.

Lightly flour a clean, flat work surface.

Scrape the dough onto the floured surface. Lightly flour your hands and finish mixing the dough by using a gentle kneading motion, working until the dough is just blended. Do not overwork the dough, you want to be certain that all of the ingredients are just blended together.

Form the dough into a disk and cover tightly in plastic wrap. Refrigerate for at least 1 hour (or up to 3 days), or until firm.

When ready to bake, preheat the oven to 350°F.

Line two baking sheets with nonstick silicone baking mats or parchment paper. (Alternatively, use nonstick baking sheets or lightly butter conventional baking sheets.) Set aside.

Remove the dough from the refrigerator and unwrap.

Place the granulated sugar on a large flat plate.

Using a tablespoon or small ice-cream scoop, make mounds of dough. Working with one piece at a time, roll the dough into balls about $1\frac{1}{2}$ inches in diameter. Using your palm, gently flatten each ball to make a puck-like shape about 2 inches in diameter. Roll each cookie in the granulated sugar to coat completely and place them, about 2 inches apart, on the prepared baking sheets.

When all of the cookies are formed, place in the oven and bake for about 10 minutes, or until just barely brown around the edges.

Remove from the oven and, using a metal spatula, transfer the cookies to wire racks to cool.

Store, airtight, at room temperature for up to a week.

**NOTE:** Dough can be stored, airtight, in the refrigerator for up to a week or in the freezer for up to a month.

# Brown Sugar-Cinnamon Crisps

By substituting light brown sugar for superfine sugar in the sugar cookie base and rolling the dough out thinly, this cookie becomes buttery and crisp. They are cinnamon graham crackers all grown up, great for snacking or dunking!

**MAKES ABOUT 2 DOZEN COOKIES**

Sugar Cookie Base Dough (page 70), substituting light brown sugar for the superfine sugar

$\frac{1}{2}$ cup ($3\frac{1}{2}$ ounces) granulated sugar

2 teaspoons ground cinnamon

Prepare the Sugar Cookie Base Dough, making the light brown sugar substitution. While the dough is still streaky, remove the bowl from the mixer and scrape the paddle clean.

Lightly flour a clean, flat work surface.

Scrape the dough onto the floured surface. Lightly flour your hands and finish mixing the dough by using a gentle kneading motion, working until the dough is just blended. Do not overwork the dough, you want to be certain that all of the ingredients are just blended together.

Form the dough into a disk and cover tightly in plastic wrap. Refrigerate for at least 1 hour (or up to 3 days), or until firm.

When ready to bake, preheat the oven to 350ºF.

Line two baking sheets with nonstick silicone baking mats or parchment paper. (Alternatively, use nonstick baking sheets or lightly butter conventional baking sheets.) Set aside.

Remove the dough from the refrigerator and unwrap.

Combine the granulated sugar and cinnamon on a large flat plate.

Lightly flour a clean, flat work surface. Place the dough in the center of the floured surface. Using a rolling pin, roll the dough out into a piece about $\frac{1}{8}$ inch thick. Using a 3-inch round fluted biscuit cutter, cut out the cookies and dip both sides in the cinnamon-sugar. Place the cookies, about 2 inches apart, on the prepared baking sheets.

When all of the cookies are formed, place in the oven and bake for about 10 minutes, or until crisp and golden brown around the edges.

Remove from the oven and, using a metal spatula, transfer the cookies to wire racks to cool.

Store, airtight, at room temperature for up to a week.

# Lemon Drop Cookies

The tart flavor of lemon in this sugar cookie brings to mind a summertime glass of frosty homemade lemonade.

**MAKES ABOUT 2 DOZEN COOKIES**

Sugar Cookie Base Dough (page 70)

2 tablespoons fresh lemon juice

2 tablespoons freshly grated lemon zest

$\frac{1}{2}$ cup (3$\frac{1}{2}$ ounces) granulated sugar

Prepare the Sugar Cookie Base Dough, adding the lemon juice and zest with the dry ingredients. While the dough is still streaky, remove the bowl from the mixer and scrape the paddle clean.

Lightly flour a clean, flat work surface.

Scrape the dough onto the floured surface. Lightly flour your hands and finish mixing the dough by using a gentle kneading motion, working until the dough is just blended. Do not overwork the dough, you want to be certain that all of the ingredients are just blended together.

Form the dough into a disk and cover tightly in plastic wrap. Refrigerate for at least 1 hour (or up to 3 days), or until firm.

When ready to bake, preheat the oven to 350°F.

Line two baking sheets with nonstick silicone baking mats or parchment paper. (Alternatively, use nonstick baking sheets or lightly butter conventional baking sheets.) Set aside.

Remove the dough from the refrigerator and unwrap. Place the granulated sugar on a large flat plate.

Using a tablespoon or small ice-cream scoop, make mounds of dough. Roll the dough into balls about 1$\frac{1}{2}$ inches in diameter. Using your palm, gently flatten each ball to make a puck-like shape about 2 inches in diameter. Roll each cookie in the granulated sugar to coat completely and place them, about 2 inches apart, on the prepared baking sheets.

When all of the cookies are formed, place in the oven and bake for about 10 minutes, or until just barely brown around the edges.

Remove from the oven and, using a metal spatula, transfer the cookies to wire racks to cool.

Store, airtight, at room temperature for up to a week.

# M&M's Sugar Cookies

This cookie has to be the all-time children's favorite, either from the bakery or when they make their own mix at one of our cookie-baking parties. I think that it is the array of bright colors in the golden dough that attracts them or perhaps it is the delicious crunch of sugar coating over melting chocolate.

**MAKES ABOUT 2 DOZEN COOKIES**

Sugar Cookie Base Dough (page 70)

2 cups (1 pound) M&M's candies

$\frac{1}{2}$ cup ($3\frac{1}{2}$ ounces) granulated sugar

Preheat the oven to 350ºF.

Line two baking sheets with nonstick silicone baking mats or parchment paper. (Alternatively, use nonstick baking sheets or lightly butter conventional baking sheets.) Set aside.

Prepare the Sugar Cookie Base Dough. While the dough is still streaky, remove the bowl from the mixer and scrape the paddle clean.

Lightly flour a clean, flat work surface.

Scrape the dough onto the floured surface. Lightly flour your hands, and finish mixing the dough by using a gentle kneading motion, working until the dough is just blended.

Using a wooden spoon, stir in the M&M's. Do not overwork the dough, you want to be certain that all of the ingredients are just blended together.

Place the granulated sugar on a large flat plate.

Using a tablespoon or small ice-cream scoop, make mounds of dough. Roll the dough into balls about $1\frac{1}{2}$ inches in diameter. Using your palm, gently flatten each ball to make a puck-like shape about 2 inches in diameter. Roll each cookie in the granulated sugar to coat completely and place them, about 2 inches apart, on the prepared baking sheets.

When all of the cookies are formed, place in the oven and bake for about 10 minutes, or until just barely brown around the edges.

Remove from the oven and, using a metal spatula, transfer the cookies to wire racks to cool.

Store, airtight, at room temperature for up to a week.

# Decorated Cut-Out Cookies

This is the basic recipe we use for all decorative cookies. It is an all-occasion recipe as cookie cutters come in every imaginable shape, style, and holiday theme. It is up to the baker (and decorator) to make them shine.

We like to add decorated cookies—even those with a simple sprinkling of sanding sugar—to party trays to bring a touch of bright color. You don't have to be a great artist to decorate; a thin coating of icing sprinkled with sparkling sanding sugar will make the cookie stand out. In fact, I think sparkling sugar is more than enough!

**MAKES ABOUT 2 DOZEN COOKIES**

**Sugar Cookie Base Dough (page 70)**

**Royal Icing (facing page)**

**Sanding sugar (optional)**

**Decorative candies such as cinnamon Red Hots, M&M's, or other candies that will withstand oven temperatures (optional)**

Prepare the Sugar Cookie Base Dough. While the dough is still streaky, remove the bowl from the mixer and scrape the paddle clean.

Lightly flour a clean, flat work surface.

Scrape the dough onto the floured surface. Lightly flour your hands and finish mixing the dough by using a gentle kneading motion, working until the dough is just blended. Do not overwork the dough, you want to be certain that all of the ingredients are just blended together.

Form the dough into a disk and cover tightly in plastic wrap. Refrigerate for at least 1 hour (or up to 3 days) , or until firm.

Line two baking sheets with nonstick silicone baking mats or parchment paper. (Alternatively, use nonstick baking sheets or lightly butter conventional baking sheets.) Set aside.

Remove the dough from the refrigerator and unwrap.

Lightly flour a clean, flat work surface. Place the dough in the center of the floured surface. Using a rolling pin, roll the dough out into a piece about $\frac{1}{4}$ inch thick. Using decorative cookie cutters, cut the dough into the desired shapes.

At this point, if not using icing, the cookies may be decorated with sanding sugar or candies, if desired.

Place the cookies, about 2 inches apart, on the prepared baking sheets.

When all of the cookies are formed, place in the refrigerator to set for 1 hour before baking.

When ready to bake, preheat the oven to 350ºF.

Remove the cookies from the refrigerator and bake in the oven for about 8 minutes, or just until barely brown around the edges.

Remove from the oven and, using a metal spatula, transfer the cookies to wire racks to cool.

If using Royal Icing, let the cookies cool completely, then decorate with the icing, sugar, and/or candies as desired.

Store, airtight, at room temperature for up to a week.

# Royal Icing

5 tablespoons meringue powder (see Note)

$\frac{1}{2}$ cup minus 2 tablespoons water

or

2 large egg whites, at room temperature

2 tablespoons water

1 tablespoon white vinegar

$4\frac{1}{2}$ cups (1 pound) confectioners' sugar, sifted

Food coloring (optional)

Combine the meringue powder and water or the egg whites, 2 tablespoons water, vinegar, and confectioners' sugar in the bowl of a standing electric mixer fitted with the paddle. Begin mixing on low speed to combine. When blended, increase the speed to medium and continue to beat for about 5 minutes, or until the icing begins to form stiff peaks. If desired, divide the icing into small amounts and stir a different shade of food coloring into each. (If not using immediately, cover the bowl with a damp, clean kitchen towel to prevent it from drying out.)

By adding more or less confectioners' sugar, the icing can be adjusted for different decorating needs. If you want the icing runny enough to easily cover the entire top of the cookie, use less confectioners' sugar. If you wish to use a pastry bag to pipe outlines or other fine details, add a little more confectioners' sugar to thicken the icing so that the details will be stiff enough to hold their shape.

NOTE: Meringue powder is available at some supermarkets, specialty food shops, and cake and bakery supply stores, and on the Internet.

# Tropical Sensation Cookies

Candied fruit adds moistness to these cookies, giving them a unique texture not usually associated with sugar cookies. The fruits stay plump and chewy after baking. You can also use chopped dried fruit, which will come out a little firmer. Both cookies are equally delicious.

**MAKES ABOUT 2 DOZEN COOKIES**

Sugar Cookie Base Dough (page 70)

2 cups (12 ounces) coarsely chopped candied papaya

2 cups (12 ounces) coarsely chopped candied pineapple

1 cup (6 ounces) shredded sweetened coconut

$\frac{1}{2}$ cup (3 ounces) shredded unsweetened coconut

Preheat the oven to 350°F.

Line two baking sheets with nonstick silicone baking mats or parchment paper. (Alternatively, use nonstick baking sheets or lightly butter conventional baking sheets.) Set aside.

Prepare the Sugar Cookie Base Dough, adding the papaya, pineapple, and sweetened coconut with the dry ingredients. While the dough is still streaky, remove the bowl from the mixer and scrape the paddle clean.

Lightly flour a clean, flat work surface.

Scrape the dough onto the floured surface. Lightly flour your hands and finish mixing the dough by using a gentle kneading motion, working until the dough is just blended. Do not overwork the dough, you want to be certain that all of the ingredients are just blended together.

Place the unsweetened coconut on a large flat plate.

Using a tablespoon or small ice-cream scoop, make mounds of dough. Roll the dough into balls about $1\frac{1}{2}$ inches in diameter. Using your palm, gently flatten each ball to make a puck-like shape about 2 inches in diameter. Roll each cookie in the unsweetened coconut to coat completely and place them, about 2 inches apart, on the prepared baking sheets.

When all of the cookies are formed, place in the oven and bake for about 10 minutes, or until just barely brown around the edges.

Remove from the oven and, using a metal spatula, transfer the cookies to wire racks to cool.

Store, airtight, at room temperature for up to a week.

# Candied Orange Cookies

A subtle and slightly refreshing flavor makes these cookies a lovely addition to a tea service. I always use a premium liqueur so that the flavor is defined and lasting in the baked cookies.

**MAKES ABOUT 2 DOZEN COOKIES**

Sugar Cookie Base Dough (page 70)

1 cup (6 ounces) chopped candied orange peel

2 tablespoons Grand Marnier or other orange-flavored liqueur

Preheat the oven to 350°F.

Line two baking sheets with nonstick silicone baking mats or parchment paper. (Alternatively, use nonstick baking sheets or lightly butter conventional baking sheets.) Set aside.

Prepare the Sugar Cookie Base Dough, adding the orange peel and liqueur with the dry ingredients. While the dough is still streaky, remove the bowl from the mixer and scrape the paddle clean.

Lightly flour a clean, flat work surface.

Scrape the dough onto the floured surface. Lightly flour your hands and finish mixing the dough by using a gentle kneading motion, working until the dough is just blended. Do not overwork the dough, you want to be certain that all of the ingredients are just blended together.

Using a tablespoon or small ice-cream scoop, make mounds of dough. Roll the dough into balls about 1½ inches in diameter. Using your palm, gently flatten each ball to make a puck-like shape about 2 inches in diameter. Place the cookies, about 2 inches apart, on the prepared baking sheets.

When all of the cookies are formed, place in the oven and bake for about 20 minutes, or until just barely brown around the edges.

Remove from the oven and, using a metal spatula, transfer the cookies to wire racks to cool.

Store, airtight, at room temperature for up to a week.

# Candied Ginger-Sugar Cookies

This cookie reminds me of a very special friend of mine, Sabena Singh, because t is one of her favorites. She has an incredible passion for exquisite foods. In her words, "I enjoy the heady flavor of ginger, especially in cookies. It conjures up memories of Masala chai and elephant rides under a blistering sun."

**MAKES ABOUT 2 DOZEN COOKIES**

Sugar Cookie Base Dough (page 70)

1 cup (6 ounces) chopped candied ginger

$\frac{1}{2}$ cup (3$\frac{1}{2}$ ounces) granulated sugar

Preheat the oven to 350°F.

Line two baking sheets with nonstick silicone baking mats or parchment paper. (Alternatively, use nonstick baking sheets or lightly butter conventional baking sheets.) Set aside.

Prepare the Sugar Cookie Base Dough, adding the ginger with the dry ingredients. While the dough is still streaky, remove the bowl from the mixer and scrape the paddle clean.

Lightly flour a clean, flat work surface.

Scrape the dough onto the floured surface. Lightly flour your hands and finish mixing the dough by using a gentle kneading motion, working until the dough is just blended. Do not overwork the dough, you want to be certain that all of the ingredients are just blended together.

Place the granulated sugar on a large flat plate.

Using a tablespoon or small ice-cream scoop, make mounds of dough. Roll the dough into balls about 1$\frac{1}{2}$ inches in diameter. Using your palm, gently flatten each ball to make a puck-like shape about 2 inches in diameter. Roll each cookie in the granulated sugar to coat completely and place them, about 2 inches apart, on the prepared baking sheets.

When all of the cookies are formed, place in the oven and bake for about 10 minutes, or until just barely brown around the edges.

Remove from the oven and, using a metal spatula, transfer the cookies to wire racks to cool.

Store, airtight, at room temperature for up to a week.

# Chestnut Cookies

I developed this cookie for a demonstration at a farmers' market tasting event in New York City's Union Square Greenmarket. I used New York City honey (yes, there are bees here) and added an unexpected touch, Italian chestnut flour. They were a big hit and sold out quickly on a very cold December Saturday.

**MAKES ABOUT 2 DOZEN COOKIES**

Sugar Cookie Base Dough (page 70), substituting 1 cup (4 ounces) chestnut flour for 1 cup (4 ounces) of the all-purpose flour

2 tablespoons good-quality honey

$\frac{1}{2}$ cup ($3\frac{1}{2}$ ounces) granulated sugar

Prepare the Sugar Cookie Base Dough, making the chestnut flour substitution and adding the honey along with the egg yolks. While the dough is still streaky, remove the bowl from the mixer and scrape the paddle clean.

Lightly flour a clean, flat work surface.

Scrape the dough onto the floured surface. Lightly flour your hands and finish mixing the dough by using a gentle kneading motion, working until the dough is just blended. Do not overwork the dough, you want to be certain that all of the ingredients are just blended together.

Form the dough into a disk and cover tightly in plastic wrap. Refrigerate for at least 1 hour (or up to 3 days), or until firm.

When ready to bake, preheat the oven to 350ºF.

Line two baking sheets with nonstick silicone baking mats or parchment paper. (Alternatively, use nonstick baking sheets or lightly butter conventional baking sheets.) Set aside.

Remove the dough from the refrigerator and unwrap.

Place the granulated sugar on a large flat plate.

Using a tablespoon or small ice-cream scoop, make mounds of dough. Roll the dough into balls about $1\frac{1}{2}$ inches in diameter. Using your palm, gently flatten each ball to make a puck-like shape about 2 inches in diameter. Roll each cookie in the granulated sugar and place them, about 2 inches apart, on the prepared baking sheets.

When all of the cookies are formed, place in the oven and bake for about 10 minutes, or until just barely brown around the edges.

Remove from the oven and, using a metal spatula, transfer the cookies to wire racks to cool.

Store, airtight, at room temperature for up to a week.

# CHAPTER 6

# SPECIAL COOKIES

# Snickerdoodles

You can find recipes for snickerdoodles in very old cookbooks. They are a Southern favorite: sugary, a little chewy, and filled with sweet spicy goodness. This is one of those recipes that needs shortening to give the baked cookie the desired texture. When I have tried using all butter, the cookies don't have the soft, chewy character that I prefer.

**MAKES ABOUT 2 DOZEN COOKIES**

$2\frac{1}{2}$ cups ($11\frac{1}{4}$ ounces) all-purpose flour

2 teaspoons cream of tartar

1 teaspoon baking soda

$\frac{1}{2}$ teaspoon salt

$\frac{1}{2}$ cup (4 ounces) unsalted butter, at room temperature

$\frac{1}{2}$ cup (4 ounces) vegetable shortening, at room temperature

$1\frac{3}{4}$ cups (12 ounces) sugar

2 large eggs, at room temperature

2 teaspoons pure vanilla extract

$\frac{1}{2}$ tablespoon ground cinnamon

Combine the flour, cream of tartar, baking soda, and salt in a mixing bowl. Set aside.

Combine the butter and shortening in the bowl of a standing electric mixer fitted with the paddle. Begin beating on low speed to blend together. Increase the speed to medium and beat for about 3 minutes, or until light and creamy.

Add $1\frac{1}{2}$ cups of the sugar in a slow steady stream and continue to beat for 2 minutes.

Reduce the speed to low and add the eggs, one at a time, scraping down the sides of the bowl with a rubber spatula after each addition. Add the vanilla and when blended, slowly beat in the dry mixture in two parts, beating until just incorporated.

Remove the bowl from the mixer, scrape down the sides of the bowl, cover tightly with plastic wrap, and refrigerate for at least 8 hours or overnight.

When ready to bake, preheat the oven to 350°F.

Combine the remaining $\frac{1}{4}$ cup sugar with the cinnamon in a large shallow bowl. Set aside.

Line two baking sheets with nonstick silicone baking mats or parchment paper. (Alternatively, use nonstick baking sheets or lightly butter conventional baking sheets.) Set aside.

Remove the dough from the refrigerator and unwrap.

Roll the dough into $1\frac{1}{4}$-inch balls. Roll each ball in the cinnamon-sugar to coat completely and place the cookies, about $2\frac{1}{2}$ inches apart, on the prepared baking sheets.

Place in the oven and bake for about 10 minutes, or until light brown. The cookies should be soft to the touch and leave a slight indentation in the center when touched. Do not overbake or they will be hard and dry.

Remove from the oven and, using a metal spatula, transfer the cookies to wire racks to cool.

Store, airtight, at room temperature for up to a week.

# S'mores

The Milk & Cookies Bakery S'mores were created by Nia, a very special intern at the bakery. She was inspired one day and the result quickly became a favorite on our list of specials.

**MAKES ABOUT 2 DOZEN COOKIES**

Unbaked Snickerdoodles dough (see page 87)

2 cups (7 ounces) mini marshmallows

2 cups (12 ounces) semisweet chocolate chips

1 cup (5 ounces) graham cracker crumbs

1 tablespoon sugar

1 teaspoon ground cinnamon

Prepare the Snickerdoodles dough. While the dough is still streaky, remove the bowl from the mixer and scrape the paddle clean.

Using a wooden spoon, stir in the mini marshmallows and chocolate chips, mixing until evenly distributed.

Scrape the dough from the bowl, pat into a flat disk, and cover tightly in plastic wrap. Refrigerate for 1 hour.

When ready to bake, preheat the oven to 350°F.

Line two baking sheets with nonstick silicone baking mats or parchment paper. (Alternatively, use nonstick baking sheets or lightly butter conventional baking sheets.) Set aside.

Combine the graham cracker crumbs with the sugar and cinnamon in a shallow bowl. Set aside.

Remove the dough from the refrigerator and unwrap.

Using your hands, form the dough into $1\frac{1}{4}$-inch balls. Roll each ball in the cinnamon-crumb-sugar to coat completely and place, about $2\frac{1}{2}$ inches apart, on the prepared baking sheets.

Place in the oven and bake for about 12 minutes, or until golden.

Remove from the oven and, using a metal spatula, transfer the cookies to wire racks to cool.

Store, airtight, at room temperature for up to a week.

# Jumbles

"Everything but the kitchen sink" could also be the name of these cookies. You can put just about anything you like into the dough and it will still be a great cookie. You might try pretzels, corn flakes, or even potato chips in place of the nuts. At Milk & Cookies Bakery, we often have these as our "special of the day"—they sell out as quickly as we can put them on the counter.

**MAKES ABOUT 2 DOZEN COOKIES**

$1\frac{1}{4}$ cups (5 ounces) all-purpose flour

1 teaspoon baking soda

$\frac{1}{4}$ teaspoon salt

$\frac{1}{2}$ cup (4 ounces) unsalted butter, at room temperature

$\frac{1}{3}$ cup plus 1 tablespoon ($2\frac{1}{2}$ ounces) granulated sugar

$\frac{1}{4}$ cup ($1\frac{3}{4}$ ounces) light brown sugar

1 large egg, at room temperature

$\frac{1}{2}$ teaspoon pure vanilla extract

1 cup (6 ounces) white chocolate chips

1 cup (4 ounces) walnut pieces

1 cup (4 ounces) coarsely chopped almonds

$\frac{1}{3}$ cup (2 ounces) raisins

Preheat the oven to 350°F.

Line two baking sheets with nonstick silicone baking mats or parchment paper. (Alternatively, use nonstick baking sheets or lightly butter conventional baking sheets.) Set aside.

Combine the flour, baking soda, and salt together in a mixing bowl. Set aside.

Put the butter in the bowl of a standing electric mixer fitted with the paddle. Begin beating on low speed. Add the granulated sugar and brown sugar, increase the speed to medium, and beat for about 4 minutes, or until light and fluffy.

Add the egg along with the vanilla, and beat to incorporate.

With the motor running, slowly add the dry ingredients, beating to combine. When the dough is well blended, remove the bowl from the mixer and scrape the paddle clean. Using a wooden spoon, stir in the chocolate chips, walnuts, almonds, and raisins, mixing until evenly distributed.

Using a tablespoon or small ice-cream scoop, place rounded mounds of the dough, about 2 inches apart, on the prepared baking sheets.

Place in the oven and bake for about 10 minutes, or until golden brown, lightly colored around the edges, and set in the center.

Remove from the oven and, using a metal spatula, transfer the cookies to wire racks to cool.

Store, airtight, at room temperature for up to a week.

# Gingersnaps

This is my favorite cookie for Christmastime. The aroma of gingersnaps baking in the oven immediately fills the kitchen with childhood holiday memories. And they are great for dipping into a tall glass of milk.

**MAKES ABOUT 2 DOZEN COOKIES**

2 cups (9 ounces) all-purpose flour, sifted

3 tablespoons ground ginger

1 teaspoon ground cinnamon

1 teaspoon baking soda

$1/4$ teaspoon ground cloves

$1/4$ teaspoon salt

$3/4$ cup (6 ounces) unsalted butter, at room temperature

$3/4$ cup (5 ounces) granulated sugar, plus 1 cup (7 ounces)

$1/2$ cup ($3^1/2$ ounces) dark brown sugar, firmly packed

1 large egg, at room temperature

1 teaspoon pure vanilla extract

1 teaspoon apple cider

Preheat the oven to 350°F.

Line two baking sheets with nonstick silicone baking mats or parchment paper. (Alternatively, use nonstick baking sheets or lightly butter conventional baking sheets.) Set aside.

Combine the flour, ginger, cinnamon, baking soda, cloves, and salt in a mixing bowl. Set aside.

Put the butter in the bowl of a standing electric mixer fitted with the paddle. Begin beating on low speed to soften. Increase the speed to medium and beat for about 3 minutes, or until light and creamy.

Add the $3/4$ cup granulated sugar and the brown sugar and beat for an additional 2 minutes.

Reduce the speed to low and add the egg. Beat to incorporate, scraping down the sides of the bowl with a rubber spatula. Beat in the vanilla and cider and when blended, slowly beat in the reserved dry mixture. When dough is just blended, remove the bowl from the mixer and scrape the paddle clean.

Place the remaining granulated sugar in a small shallow bowl.

Using your hands, roll the dough into balls about 1 inch in diameter. Roll each ball in the sugar to coat completely and place them, about 2 inches apart, on the prepared baking sheets.

When all of the cookies have been formed, place in the oven and bake for about 12 minutes, or until lightly colored.

Remove from the oven and, using a metal spatula, transfer the cookies to wire racks to cool.

Store, airtight, at room temperature for up to a week.

# Coconut Macaroons

Too often, macaroons are just too sweet. My solution is to add cocoa nibs to the recipe. They offset the sweetness, add an extra texture, and marry well with the coconut.

**MAKES ABOUT 2 DOZEN COOKIES**

1 cup (6 ounces) shredded unsweetened coconut flakes

1 cup (3 ounces) shredded sweetened coconut flakes

½ cup (2 ounces) cocoa nibs

¾ cup (5 ounces) sugar

3 egg whites, at room temperature

2 tablespoons pure vanilla extract

DIPPING CHOCOLATE

2 cups (12 ounces) dark couverture chocolate, chopped (see Note)

¼ cup vegetable oil

Preheat the oven to 325°F.

Line two baking sheets with nonstick silicone baking mats or parchment paper. (Alternatively, use nonstick baking sheets or lightly butter conventional baking sheets.) Set aside.

Combine the unsweetened coconut and sweetened coconut with the cocoa nibs in a mixing bowl, stirring to blend. Set aside.

Combine the sugar and egg whites in the top of a double boiler over simmering water. Cook, stirring constantly, until the sugar has melted into the egg whites. Add the reserved coconut mixture along with the vanilla and stir to combine.

Using a tablespoon or small ice-cream scoop, make small, neat mounds of dough, place them at least 1 inch apart, on the prepared baking sheets.

Place in the oven and bake for about 12 minutes, or until golden brown around the edges.

Remove from the oven and, using a metal spatula, transfer the cookies to wire racks to cool.

To prepare the dipping chocolate: Place the chocolate in the top of a double boiler over simmering water. Cook, stirring occasionally, until the chocolate has melted completely.

Add the vegetable oil and, using a whisk, beat to emulsify.

Remove from the heat and let rest for 10 minutes.

Working with one cookie at a time, fix the bottom of the macaroon onto the tines of a fork and carefully dip the top of the macaroon into the warm chocolate or hold the cookie and dip half in. Hold the macaroon over the chocolate so the excess can drip back into the pan.

Place the macaroons, flat-side down, on a wire rack to set.

Store in layers separated by waxed paper, airtight, at room temperature for up to a week.

**NOTE:** Couverture or coating chocolate is a high-quality chocolate made specifically for coating candies. It's available at some specialty food shops and cake and bakery supply stores, and on the Internet.

# Mocha-Cherry Drops

I learned to make these cookies at one of the first restaurant jobs I had away from home. I was drawn to them because they reminded me of a cookie that I loved from a hometown bakery. Over time, I added nuts and a little more cocoa to make them a bit richer. They remain one of my (many!) favorites.

**MAKES ABOUT 2 DOZEN COOKIES**

$\frac{1}{2}$ cup (3 ounces) dried cherries

2 cups (8 ounces) all-purpose flour

1 tablespoon Dutch-processed cocoa powder

2 teaspoons espresso powder or pure coffee extract

$\frac{1}{4}$ teaspoon salt

1 cup (8 ounces) unsalted butter, at room temperature

$\frac{1}{2}$ cup ($3\frac{1}{2}$ ounces) sugar

1 teaspoon pure vanilla extract

1 cup (4 ounces) walnut pieces

Put the cherries in a small heatproof container with boiling water to cover. Set aside to rehydrate for about 10 minutes.

Combine the flour, cocoa powder, espresso powder, and salt in a mixing bowl. Set aside.

Put the butter in the bowl of a standing electric mixer fitted with the paddle. Begin beating on low speed. Add the sugar and increase the speed to medium. Beat for about 3 minutes, or until light and fluffy. Beat in the vanilla.

Reduce the speed to low and add the flour mixture, scraping down the sides of the bowl with a rubber spatula. While the dough is still streaky, remove the bowl from the mixer and scrape the paddle clean.

Drain the cherries thoroughly and, using a chef's knife, chop them into small pieces.

Using a wooden spoon, stir the walnuts and cherries into the dough, beating until evenly distributed. You can also do this in the mixer, but heavy mixing tends to break up the nuts and the result is a less chunky and drier cookie.

Using your hands, form the dough into 1-inch balls and place them, about 2 inches apart, on the prepared baking sheets.

Place in the oven and bake for about 10 minutes, or until lightly colored and set in the center.

Remove from the oven and, using a metal spatula, transfer the cookies to wire racks to cool.

Store, airtight, at room temperature for up to a week.

# Chocolate-Macadamia Nut Cookies

These easy-to-make cookies are terrific to prepare in advance and keep in the freezer for the moment when a quick dessert or snack is needed. After baking and cooling, the texture should be just a little bit crisp.

**MAKES ABOUT 2 DOZEN COOKIES**

$1^1/_2$ cups (6 ounces) al -purpose flour

$1/_2$ cup ($1^3/_4$ ounces) Dutch-processed cocoa powder

2 teaspoons baking soca

$3/_4$ teaspoon salt

$3/_4$ cup (6 ounces) unsalted butter, at room temperature

$1/_2$ cup ($3^1/_2$ ounces) light brown sugar

$1/_2$ cup ($3^1/_2$ ounces) granulated sugar

1 large egg, at room temperature

$1/_2$ cup (2 ounces) chopped macadamia nuts

Combine the flour, cocoa powder, baking soda, and salt in a mixing bowl. Set aside.

Put the butter in the bowl of a standing electric mixer fitted with the paddle. Begin beating on low speed. Increase the speed to medium and beat for about 3 minutes, or until light and creamy.

Add the brown sugar and granulated sugar and beat for an additional 2 minutes.

Reduce the speed to low and add the egg. Beat to incorporate, scraping down the sides of the bowl with a rubber spatula. While the dough is still a bit streaky, remove the bowl from the mixer and scrape the paddle clean.

Using a wooden spoon, stir the nuts into the dough, beating until evenly distributed. You can also do this in the mixer, but heavy mixing tends to break up the nuts and the result is a less chunky cookie.

Divide the dough into two equal pieces. Roll each piece into a log about 2 inches in diameter. Cover tightly in plastic wrap and place in the refrigerator for about 1 hour, or until well chilled.

When ready to bake, preheat the oven to 350°F.

Line two baking sheets with nonstick silicone baking mats or parchment paper. (Alternatively, use nonstick baking sheets or lightly butter conventional baking sheets.) Set aside.

Remove the chilled dough from the refrigerator and unwrap. Using a sharp knife, cut each log, crosswise, into slices about $1/_2$ inch thick. Place the cookies, at least 1 inch apart, on the prepared baking sheets.

Place in the oven and bake for about 12 minutes, or until golden.

Remove from the oven and, using a metal spatula, transfer the cookies to wire racks to cool.

Store, airtight, at room temperature for up to a week.

# Maple-Pecan Cookies

Quite similar to the very popular boxed pecan sandies, these are buttery and melt-in-your-mouth cookies. I love them with an aromatic herbal tea.

**MAKES ABOUT 4 DOZEN COOKIES**

$3/4$ cup (6 ounces) unsalted butter

2 cups (9 ounces) all-purpose flour, sifted

$1/4$ teaspoon baking soda

$1/4$ teaspoon salt

$2/3$ cup pure maple syrup

2 large eggs, at room temperature

2 tablespoons fresh orange juice

$1/2$ tablespoon pure vanilla extract

1 teaspoon maple-flavored extract

$3/4$ cup (5 ounces) granulated sugar

$1/2$ cup ($3 1/2$ ounces) light brown sugar, firmly packed

1 tablespoon molasses

$1 1/2$ cups (6 ounces) coarsely chopped toasted pecans

Preheat the oven to 350°F.

Line two baking sheets with nonstick silicone baking mats or parchment paper. (Alternatively, use nonstick baking sheets or lightly butter conventional baking sheets.) Set aside.

Put the butter in a small saucepan over low heat. Heat until just melted. Remove from the heat, pour into a mixing bowl, and set aside to cool.

Combine the flour, baking soda, and salt in a mixing bowl. Set aside.

Using a wooden spoon, stir the maple syrup into the cooled butter. When blended, stir in the eggs and orange juice along with the vanilla and maple extract.

Using a whisk, beat in the granulated sugar and brown sugar along with the molasses, whisking until the batter is smooth and lump free.

Using the wooden spoon, add the reserved flour mixture in thirds, beating just to blend. When blended, fold in the nuts.

Using a tablespoon or small ice-cream scoop, drop the dough in mounds, about 2 inches apart, onto the prepared baking sheets.

Place in the oven and bake for 8 minutes, or until golden brown.

Remove from the oven and, using a metal spatula, transfer the cookies to wire racks to cool.

Store, airtight, at room temperature for up to a week.

# Belgian Nut Cookies

Do you remember those store-bought cookies shaped like a windmill? Well, these cookies will bring back memories. They have the perfect combination of sugar and spice to capture the taste and aroma of those old-fashioned favorites.

**MAKES ABOUT 50 COOKIES**

$^{2}/_{3}$ cup (5 ounces) unsalted butter

$^{2}/_{3}$ cup (5 ounces) vegetable shortening

$4^{1}/_{2}$ cups ($1^{1}/_{4}$ pounds) bread flour, sifted

1 teaspoon baking powder

1 teaspoon baking soda

$^{1}/_{2}$ cup plus 5 tablespoons (6 ounces) granulated sugar

$^{1}/_{2}$ cup plus 5 tablespoons (6 ounces) light brown sugar, firmly packed

1 teaspoon ground cinnamon

$^{1}/_{2}$ teaspoon salt

1 teaspoon pure vanilla extract

5 large eggs, at room temperature

2 cups (8 ounces) sliced almonds

Lightly coat a $17^{1}/_{4}$-by-$11^{1}/_{2}$-by-1-inch jelly-roll pan with nonstick vegetable spray. Lay a piece of parchment paper in the greased pan, taking care that it fits neatly at the sides and corners. Set aside.

Put the butter and shortening in a small saucepan over low heat. Heat just until melted. Remove from the heat and set aside to cool.

Combine the flour, baking powder, and baking soda in a mixing bowl. Set aside.

Combine the granulated sugar and brown sugar with the cinnamon, salt, and vanilla in a mixing bowl, beating with a wooden spoon to blend. When blended, beat in the melted butter and shortening. When the sugar mixture is smooth, beat in the eggs, followed by the almonds. When completely blended, beat in the reserved flour mixture to just incorporate.

Scrape the mixture into the prepared pan and spread it out in a neat, even layer that is $^{1}/_{4}$ inch thick. It should just about fill the pan. Cover with plastic wrap and transfer to the freezer. Freeze completely.

When ready to bake, preheat the oven to 350°F.

Line two baking sheets with nonstick silicone baking mats or parchment paper. (Alternatively, use nonstick baking sheets or lightly butter conventional baking sheets.) Set aside.

Flip the chilled dough out of the pan onto a cutting board. Starting at the $11^{1}/_{2}$-inch edge, use a pastry cutter or small, sharp knife and cut the dough into strips approximately 3 inches wide. Cut each strip crosswise into rectangles.

As they are cut, place the cookies on the prepared baking sheets. Place in the oven and bake for about 7 minutes, or until light brown around the edges.

Remove from the oven and, using a metal spatula, transfer the cookies to wire racks to cool.

Store, airtight, at room temperature for up to a week.

# Pumpkin-Cranberry Cookies

Don't feel like making a pie for the Thanksgiving table? These cookies are an easy alternative and they absolutely fill the house with the aromas of the season. They are good keepers so you can make them a couple of days ahead to save time on that monumental cooking day.

**MAKES ABOUT 4 DOZEN COOKIES**

2 cups (8 ounces) all-purpose flour

1 teaspoon baking powder

$\frac{1}{2}$ teaspoon baking soda

$\frac{1}{2}$ teaspoon salt

$\frac{1}{2}$ tablespoon plus 1 teaspoon ground cinnamon

$\frac{1}{2}$ teaspoon ground nutmeg

$\frac{1}{2}$ teaspoon ground cloves

1 cup (8 ounces) unsalted butter, at room temperature

1 cup (7 ounces) sugar

1 teaspoon pure vanilla extract

1 large egg, at room temperature

1 cup (8 ounces) pumpkin puree

1 cup (6 ounces) fresh cranberries

Preheat the oven to 350ºF.

Line two baking sheets with nonstick silicone baking mats or parchment paper. (Alternatively, use nonstick baking sheets or lightly butter conventional baking sheets.) Set aside.

Combine the flour, baking powder, baking soda, and salt in a bowl. Add the cinnamon, nutmeg, and cloves and sift all together into a mixing bowl. Set aside.

Put the butter in the bowl of a standing electric mixer fitted with the paddle. Begin beating on low speed. Add the sugar, increase the speed to medium, and beat for about 4 minutes, or until light and fluffy. Beat in the vanilla. Add the egg, beating to incorporate, then add the pumpkin puree and beat to blend well.

With the motor running, slowly add the dry ingredients, beating to combine. When the dough is just blended, remove the bowl from the mixer and scrape the paddle clean. Stirring with a wooden spoon, beat in the cranberries until evenly distributed.

Using a tablespoon or small ice-cream scoop, place rounded mounds of the dough, about 2 inches apart, on the prepared baking sheets. Place in the oven and bake for about 10 minutes, or until set in the center and lightly colored around the edges. They should feel cakelike and the center should spring back when lightly touched.

Remove from the oven and, using a metal spatula, transfer the cookies to wire racks to cool.

Store, airtight, at room temperature for up to a week.

**VARIATION:** At Milk & Cookies Bakery, in the fall we use these cookies to make Pumpkin Whoopie Pies. Roll the dough into balls, about the size of a large walnut. Place the balls, about 2 inches apart, on the prepared baking sheets. Working with one cookie at a time, press down on each ball with the bottom of a drinking glass to form a disk about $\frac{1}{8}$ inch thick. Bake as directed. When cool, spread about 2 tablespoons Vanilla Cream Filling (page 109) on the flat side of a cookie. Top with a second cookie, flat-side down, and press together gently. Set aside for about 15 minutes before serving or storing.

# Gingerbread Cookies

I use this recipe to make gingerbread men and other cut-out cookies. It is a very firm dough that holds its shape and will not spread when baked. If you wish to decorate these cookies, use Royal Icing (page 77).

**MAKES ABOUT 2 DOZEN COOKIES**

$2\frac{1}{4}$ cups (10 ounces) all-purpose flour, sifted

$\frac{1}{4}$ teaspoon baking powder

$\frac{1}{4}$ teaspoon salt

1 large egg, at room temperature

1 egg white, at room temperature

$\frac{1}{4}$ cup (2 ounces) unsalted butter, at room temperature

$\frac{1}{2}$ cup ($3\frac{1}{2}$ ounces) granulated sugar

$\frac{1}{3}$ cup ($2\frac{1}{4}$ ounces) light brown sugar

2 tablespoons molasses

$\frac{1}{4}$ teaspoon ground ginger

$\frac{1}{4}$ teaspoon ground cinnamon

Combine the flour, baking powder, and salt in a mixing bowl. Set aside.

Combine the egg and egg white in a small bowl, whisking to blend. Set aside.

Put the butter in the bowl of a standing electric mixer fitted with the paddle. Begin beating on low speed. Increase the speed to medium and beat for about 3 minutes, or until light and creamy.

Add the granulated sugar and brown sugar along with the molasses, ginger, and cinnamon and continue to beat for 3 minutes.

Reduce the speed to low and add the egg mixture, scraping down the sides of the bowl with a rubber spatula. When the dough is well-blended, remove the bowl from the mixer and scrape the paddle clean.

Divide the dough in half and form each piece into a disk. Cover each disk tightly in plastic wrap and refrigerate for at least 1 hour or up to 24 hours to chill thoroughly.

When ready to bake, preheat the oven to 350°F.

Line two baking sheets with nonstick silicone baking mats or parchment paper. (Alternatively, use nonstick baking sheets or lightly butter conventional baking sheets.) Set aside.

Lightly flour a clean, flat work surface.

Remove one piece of the dough from the refrigerator. Unwrap it and place on the floured surface.

With a rolling pin, roll the dough out to about $\frac{1}{4}$ inch thick. Cut out the cookies using cutters or other forms. Using an offset spatula, place the cut-out cookies, about 1 inch apart, on the prepared baking sheets. Repeat with the remaining piece of dough.

When all of the cookies are formed, transfer to the refrigerator to chill for about 15 minutes before baking. This final chill helps the cookies keep their shape during baking.

Remove from the refrigerator and place in the oven. Bake for about 15 minutes, or just until slightly colored around the edges.

Remove from the oven and, using a metal spatula, transfer the cookies to wire racks to cool.

Store, airtight, at room temperature for up to a week.

**NOTE:** If you want a high sheen on the finished cookies, lightly coat them with egg wash (see Note, page 157) before baking.

# Chewy Chocolate Chip Cookies

The addition of chocolate syrup to the dough makes these cookies very fudgy and moist. They are good keepers, staying soft and chewy for at least a week.

**MAKES ABOUT 2 DOZEN COOKIES**

$2\frac{1}{2}$ cups ($11\frac{1}{4}$ ounces) all-purpose flour

1 teaspoon baking soda

$\frac{1}{2}$ teaspoon salt

$\frac{1}{2}$ cup (4 ounces) unsalted butter, at room temperature

1 cup (7 ounces) light brown sugar, firmly packed

$\frac{1}{2}$ cup ($3\frac{1}{2}$ ounces) granulated sugar

$\frac{1}{3}$ cup chocolate syrup

2 tablespoons light corn syrup

2 large eggs, at room temperature

2 teaspoons pure vanilla extract

2 cups (12 ounces) semisweet chocolate chips

Preheat the oven to 350ºF.

Line two baking sheets with nonstick silicone baking mats or parchment paper. (Alternatively, use nonstick baking sheets or lightly butter conventional baking sheets.) Set aside.

Combine the flour, baking soda, and salt in a mixing bowl. Set aside.

Put the butter in the bowl of a standing electric mixer fitted with the paddle. Begin beating on low speed. Increase the speed to medium and beat for about 3 minutes, or until light and creamy.

With the motor running, gradually add the brown sugar and granulated sugar along with the chocolate syrup and corn syrup, beating until very light and creamy.

Add the eggs, one at a time, and beat to incorporate. Beat in the vanilla and when blended, add the reserved dry mixture, beating to just combine. While the dough is still streaky, remove the bowl from the mixer and scrape the paddle clean. Using a wooden spoon, stir in the chocolate chips until evenly distributed.

Using a tablespoon or small ice-cream scoop, place mounds of the dough, about 2 inches apart, on the prepared baking sheets. Place in the oven and bake for about 12 minutes, or until brown and crisp around the edges and set in the center.

Remove from the oven and, using a metal spatula, transfer the cookies to wire racks to cool.

Store, airtight, at room temperature for up to a week.

# Chocolate Sablé Cookies

This is a simple chocolate version of the classic French sablé. By combining with the Orange Sablé Cookie dough (see facing page), you can make a checkerboard or spiral cookie that is an interesting addition to any cookie plate.

**MAKES ABOUT 4 DOZEN COOKIES**

¾ cup plus 2 tablespoons (7 ounces) unsalted butter, at room temperature

1 cup (3½ ounces) confectioners' sugar, sifted

½ cup (2 ounces) almond flour

1 large egg, at room temperature

1 tablespoon pure vanilla extract

Pinch of salt

2 cups (8 ounces) cake flour, sifted

2 tablespoons Dutch-processed cocoa powder

Put the butter in the bowl of a standing electric mixer fitted with the paddle. Begin beating on low speed. Add the confectioners' sugar and almond flour and increase the speed to medium. Beat for about 3 minutes, or until light and fluffy. Add the egg, vanilla, and salt and beat until well blended.

Reduce the speed to low and add the cake flour and cocoa powder, scraping down the sides of the bowl with a rubber spatula. When the dough is just blended, remove the bowl from the mixer and scrape the paddle clean.

Using your hands, form the dough into a log about 1½ inches in diameter. Cover the log tightly in plastic wrap and refrigerate for 1 hour.

When ready to bake, preheat the oven to 350°F.

Line two baking sheets with nonstick silicone baking mats or parchment paper. (Alternatively, use nonstick baking sheets or lightly butter conventional baking sheets.) Set aside.

Remove the log from the refrigerator and unwrap. Using a sharp knife, cut the log, crosswise, into ¼-inch-thick slices and place them, about 2 inches apart, on the prepared baking sheets.

Place in the oven and bake for about 10 minutes, or until lightly colored.

Remove from the oven and, using a metal spatula, transfer the cookies to wire racks to cool.

Store, airtight, at room temperature for up to a week.

**VARIATION:** To make checkerboard or spiral cookies, you will need two contrasting colors of dough. Roll each refrigerated dough log to a ½-inch thickness. Brush one layer with egg wash (see Note, page 157), place the second layer on top, and press gently to adhere.

For a checkerboard, trim the edges of the sandwiched dough so you have a neat rectangle. Cut your rectangle into ½-inch-thick strips. Place three strips side-by-side on a clean piece of plastic wrap. Brush with egg wash, then top with three additional strips so you have a black-and-white checkerboard pattern. Rewrap and freeze for 15 minutes, then slice and bake as instructed.

For a spiral, starting at the edge farthest from your body, roll the dough (like a jellyroll) into a firm tube. Tuck the edges under. Rewrap and freeze for 15 minutes, then slice and bake as instructed.

# Orange Sablé Cookies

This is a classic butter cookie with just a hint of orange. It makes a wonderful addition to an afternoon tea plate.

**MAKES ABOUT 2 DOZEN COOKIES**

½ cup plus 2 tablespoons (5 ounces) unsalted butter, at room temperature

1 cup (3½ ounces) confectioners' sugar, sifted

½ cup (2 ounces) almond flour (see Note)

1 large egg, at room temperature

Zest of 1 orange

Pinch of salt

1½ cups (6 ounces) cake flour, sifted

½ cup (3½ ounces) granulated sugar

Put the butter in the bowl of a standing electric mixer fitted with the paddle. Begin beating on low speed. Add the confectioners' sugar and almond flour and increase the speed to medium. Beat for about 3 minutes, or until light and fluffy. Add the egg, orange zest, and salt and beat until well blended.

Reduce the speed to low and add the cake flour, scraping down the sides of the bowl with a rubber spatula. When the dough is just blended, remove the bowl from the mixer and scrape the paddle clean.

Using your hands, form the dough into a log about 1½ inches in diameter. Cover the log tightly in plastic wrap and refrigerate for 1 hour.

When ready to bake, preheat the oven to 350°F.

Line two baking sheets with nonstick silicone baking mats or parchment paper. (Alternatively, use nonstick baking sheets or lightly butter conventional baking sheets.) Set aside.

Place the granulated sugar on a large flat plate.

Put a little cool water in a small bowl.

Remove the log from the refrigerator and unwrap. Using a pastry brush, lightly brush the log with the water and immediately roll the log in the sugar.

Using a sharp knife, cut the log, crosswise, into ¼-inch-thick slices and place the slices, about 2 inches apart, on the prepared baking sheets.

Place in the oven and bake for about 10 minutes, or until lightly colored.

Remove from the oven and, using a metal spatula, transfer the cookies to wire racks to cool.

Store, airtight, at room temperature for up to a week.

**NOTE:** To make Chestnut-Orange Sablé Cookies, replace the almond flour with the same amount of chestnut flour.

# Carrot Cake Cookies

These sandwich cookies have an unexpected cakelike texture. They are a terrific alternative to making this much-loved cake. It is one of our most-requested recipes.

**MAKES 1 DOZEN SANDWICH COOKIES**

2 cups (8 ounces) all-purpose flour

1 teaspoon baking powder

1 teaspoon baking soda

1 teaspoon ground cinnamon

$\frac{1}{2}$ teaspoon ground nutmeg

$\frac{1}{4}$ teaspoon salt

1 cup (8 ounces) unsalted butter, at room temperature

1 cup (7 ounces) light brown sugar, firmly packed

1 cup (7 ounces) granulated sugar

2 large eggs, at room temperature

1 teaspoon pure vanilla extract

2 cups (6 ounces) old-fashioned rolled oats

$2\frac{1}{2}$ cups (8 ounces) finely grated carrots

1 cup (6 ounces) raisins

Cream Cheese Filling (facing page)

Preheat the oven to 350°F.

Line two baking sheets with nonstick silicone baking mats or parchment paper. (Alternatively, use nonstick baking sheets or lightly butter conventional baking sheets.) Set aside.

Combine the flour, baking powder, baking soda, cinnamon, nutmeg, and salt in a mixing bowl. Set aside.

Put the butter in the bowl of a standing electric mixer fitted with the paddle. Begin beating on low speed. Increase the speed to medium and beat for about 3 minutes, or until light and creamy. With the motor running, gradually add the brown sugar and granulated sugar, beating until very light and creamy.

Add the eggs, one at a time, and beat to incorporate. Beat in the vanilla and when blended, gradually add the reserved dry ingredients along with the oats, beating until completely incorporated. While the dough is still streaky, remove the bowl from the mixer and scrape the paddle clean. Using a wooden spoon, stir in the carrots and raisins until evenly distributed.

Using a tablespoon or small ice cream scoop, place mounds of the dough, about 2 inches apart, on the prepared baking sheets. Place in the oven and bake for about 15 minutes, or until brown and crisp around the edges and set in the center.

Remove from the oven and, using a metal spatula, transfer the cookies to wire racks to cool.

When cool, make the cookie sandwiches. Using an offset spatula, spread about 2 tablespoons of the Cream Cheese filling on the flat side of a cookie. Top with a second cookie, flat-side down, and press together gently.

When all of the cookie sandwiches have been made, store, airtight in layers separated by waxed paper, at room temperature for up to a week.

# Cream Cheese Filling

2 cups (1 pound) cream cheese, at room temperature

$^{2}/_{3}$ cup (2 ounces) confectioners' sugar

$^{1}/_{2}$ teaspoon ground ginger

$^{1}/_{4}$ teaspoon ground allspice

$^{3}/_{4}$ teaspoon pure vanilla extract

Put the cream cheese in the bowl of a standing electric mixer fitted with the paddle. Begin beating on low speed. Increase the speed to medium and beat for about 3 minutes, or until light and creamy.

With the motor running, add the confectioners' sugar, ginger, and allspice, beating until very light and fluffy. Beat in the vanilla.

Store, airtight, in the refrigerator for up to a week.

# Peanut Butter Cream-Filled Wafer Cookies

The "bread" part of these sandwiches is a very thin, crisp wafer that holds up well to the creamy filling. They taste best when the cookie remains crisp, so fill them just before serving. If you hold them for too long in the refrigerator or at room temperature, the cookies will soften and break apart.

**MAKES 1 DOZEN SANDWICH COOKIES**

1 cup (8 ounces) unsalted butter, at room temperature

1½ cups (10½ ounces) sugar

2 large eggs, at room temperature

3 cups (9 ounces) old-fashioned rolled oats

1 teaspoon salt

2 teaspoons pure vanilla extract

½ cup (2 ounces) chopped roasted, skinless peanuts

Peanut Butter Filling (facing page)

Preheat the oven to 350ºF.

Line two baking sheets with nonstick silicone baking mats or parchment paper. (Alternatively, use nonstick baking sheets or lightly butter conventional baking sheets.) Set aside.

Put the butter in the bowl of a standing electric mixer fitted with the paddle. Begin beating on low speed. Add the sugar, increase the speed to medium, and beat for about 4 minutes, or until light and fluffy.

Add the eggs, one at a time, beating to incorporate.

With the motor running, slowly add the oats and salt, beating to combine. When blended, beat in the vanilla followed by the peanuts, beating until incorporated. When the dough is just blended, remove the bowl from the mixer and scrape the paddle clean.

Using your hands, roll the dough into balls about the size of a large walnut. Place the balls, about 2 inches apart, on the prepared baking sheets. Working with one cookie at a time, press down on each ball with the bottom of a drinking glass to form a disk about ⅛ inch thick.

When all of the cookies have been made, place in the oven and bake for about 8 minutes, or until golden brown. The cookies should spread quite a bit and be completely browned. Don't fret if the edges get dark brown; they will be trimmed off.

Remove from the oven and, using a 3-inch round biscuit cutter, immediately cut each cookie to remove the darker edge and make a neat circle. Using a metal spatula, transfer the cookies to wire racks to cool completely.

Store, airtight, at room temperature for up to a week.

About 15 minutes before serving, spread about 2 tablespoons of the filling on the flat side of a cookie. Top with a second cookie, flat-side down, and press together gently.

# Peanut Butter Filling

1 cup (8 ounces) smooth peanut butter

$\frac{1}{2}$ cup (4 ounces) unsalted butter,
at room temperature

$\frac{1}{4}$ cup honey

Combine the peanut butter and butter in the bowl of a standing electric mixer fitted with the paddle. Begin beating on low speed. Add the honey, increase the speed to medium, and beat for about 3 minutes, or until light and fluffy.

Store, airtight, in the refrigerator for up to a week.

# Vanilla Cream-Filled Chocolate Sandwich Cookies

With these cookies, you are almost compelled to pull them apart and lick the yummy cream off first, then enjoy the delicious chocolate cookie.

**MAKES ABOUT 1 DOZEN SANDWICH COOKIES**

$1\frac{1}{4}$ cups (5 ounces) all-purpose flour

$\frac{1}{2}$ cup (2 ounces) Dutch-processed cocoa powder, plus $\frac{1}{4}$ cup (1 ounce)

1 teaspoon baking soda

$\frac{1}{4}$ teaspoon baking powder

$\frac{1}{2}$ cup plus 2 tablespoons (5 ounces) unsalted butter, at room temperature

$1\frac{1}{2}$ cups ($10\frac{1}{2}$ ounces) sugar

1 large egg, at room temperature

Vanilla Cream Filling (facing page)


Preheat the oven to 350ºF.

Line two baking sheets with nonstick silicone baking mats or parchment paper. (Alternatively, use nonstick baking sheets or lightly butter conventional baking sheets.) Set aside.

Combine the flour, $\frac{1}{2}$ cup cocoa, baking soda, and baking powder together in a mixing bowl. Set aside.

Put the butter in the bowl of a standing electric mixer fitted with the paddle. Begin beating on low speed. Add the sugar, increase the speed to medium, and beat for about 4 minutes, or until light and fluffy.

Add the egg, beating to incorporate.

With the motor running, slowly add the dry ingredients, beating to combine. When the dough is just blended, remove the bowl from the mixer and scrape the paddle clean.

Using your hands, roll the dough into balls about the size of a large walnut. Place the balls, about 2 inches apart, on the prepared baking sheets. Using your palm, gently flatten each ball to make a puck-like shape, about 2 inches in diameter.

Place the remaining $\frac{1}{4}$ cup cocoa in a shallow container. For each cookie, dip the bottom of a drinking glass into the cocoa and press down to flatten each ball into a disk about $\frac{1}{8}$ inch thick.

Place in the oven and bake for about 10 minutes, or until lightly colored around the edges and firm in the center.

Remove from the oven and, using a metal spatula, transfer the cookies to wire racks to cool completely.

Spread about 2 tablespoons of the filling on the flat side of a cookie. Top with a second cookie, flat-side down, and press together gently. Set aside for about 15 minutes before serving or storing.

Store, airtight, at room temperature for up to a week.

# Vanilla Cream Filling

$\frac{1}{2}$ cup (4 ounces) unsalted butter, at room temperature

$\frac{1}{2}$ cup (4 ounces) vegetable shortening

4 cups (14 ounces) confectioners' sugar, sifted

1 tablespoon plus 1 teaspoon pure vanilla extract

Combine the butter and shortening in the bowl of a standing electric mixer fitted with the paddle. Begin beating on low speed. Add the sugar, increase the speed to medium, and beat for about 4 minutes, or until light and fluffy. Beat in the vanilla.

Store, airtight, in the refrigerator for up to 2 weeks.

# Ice-Cream Sandwich Cookies

These cookies will remind you of the good ol' ice-cream truck and the ice-cream cookie that stuck to your fingers as soon as you opened the wrapping. They usually had vanilla ice cream, but I always looked for one with Neapolitan filling, stripes of chocolate, vanilla, and strawberry. Nowadays, I fill them with a variety of flavors, with crunchy candies and cookie dough fillings.

**MAKES 1 DOZEN SANDWICH COOKIES**

1 cup plus 1 tablespoon ($4\frac{1}{2}$ ounces) all-purpose flour

2 tablespoons Dutch-processed cocoa powder

$\frac{1}{2}$ teaspoon baking powder

$\frac{1}{4}$ teaspoon ground cinnamon

$\frac{1}{4}$ teaspoon salt

$\frac{1}{2}$ cup plus 1 tablespoon ($4\frac{1}{2}$ ounces) unsalted butter, at room temperature

$\frac{1}{2}$ cup (3 ounces) chopped bittersweet chocolate

1 large egg, at room temperature

$\frac{1}{2}$ cup ($3\frac{1}{2}$ ounces) sugar

1 teaspoon pure vanilla extract

1 tablespoon pure coffee extract

2 quarts ice cream of choice, slightly softened

Preheat the oven to 350°F.

Lightly coat a $17\frac{1}{4}$-by-$11\frac{1}{2}$-by-1-inch jelly-roll pan with nonstick vegetable spray. Lay a piece of parchment paper in the greased pan, taking care that it fits neatly at the sides and corners. Set aside.

Combine the flour, cocoa, baking powder, cinnamon, and salt in a mixing bowl. Set aside.

Combine the butter with the chocolate in the top of a double boiler over simmering water. Heat, stirring frequently, for about 5 minutes, or until the chocolate and butter have melted and blended together. Remove from the heat and set aside.

Put the egg in the bowl of a standing electric mixer fitted with the whisk. Begin whipping on medium speed until the egg is light and fluffy and falls from the whisk in a ribbon. Increase the speed and beat for 1 minute. With the motor running, begin slowly adding the sugar and beat until the mixture forms a soft ribbon when lifted from the bowl.

Lower the speed to medium and, with the motor running, beat in the reserved chocolate mixture along with the vanilla and coffee extract.

When combined, add the dry ingredients and beat to just combine.

Scrape the batter into the prepared pan, and using an offset spatula, spread it in a thin, even layer. Place in the oven. Bake for about 8 minutes, or until the edges begin to pull away from the sides of the pan. The batter should look dry and no longer be shiny.

Remove from the oven and using a sharp knife, immediately cut into $2\frac{1}{2}$-inch squares or use cookie cutters to make other shapes. Don't let it cool too much or it will become too crisp and difficult to cut.

Allow to cool completely before assembling the sandwiches.

Spread about $\frac{1}{4}$ cup of the ice cream on the flat side of a cookie. Top with a second cookie, flat-side down, and press together gently. Immediately transfer to the freezer to set.

When set, wrap up each sandwich individually in plastic wrap and freezer paper, and store for up to 3 weeks in the freezer.

CHAPTER 7

# FAMILY FAVORITES

# Biscotti

This classic biscotti recipe welcomes the addition of any type of nut or dried fruit that you want. It always works.

Biscotti dough should be on the wet side because this moisture is what will give biscotti their dry, airy texture after they've been baked and toasted.

**MAKES ABOUT 50 COOKIES**

4 cups (1 pound) all-purpose flour

1 teaspoon baking powder

$1/3$ cup (3 ounces) unsalted butter, at room temperature

$2/3$ cup ($4 1/2$ ounces) granulated sugar

$2/3$ cup ($4 1/2$ ounces) light brown sugar

4 large eggs, at room temperature

1 teaspoon pure vanilla extract

1 teaspoon almond extract

Preheat the oven to 350ºF.

Line two baking sheets with nonstick silicone baking mats or parchment paper. (Alternatively, use nonstick baking sheets or lightly butter conventional baking sheets.) Set aside.

Combine the flour and baking powder in a mixing bowl. Set aside.

Put the butter in the bowl of a standing electric mixer fitted with the paddle. Begin beating on low speed. Add the granulated sugar and brown sugar, increase the speed to medium, and beat for about 4 minutes, or until light and fluffy.

Add the eggs, one at a time, beating to incorporate. Beat in the vanilla and almond extract.

When combined, add the dry ingredients and beat to combine. When the dough is just blended, remove the bowl from the mixer and scrape the paddle clean.

Divide the dough into two equal pieces and then form each piece into a log about 10 inches long and $1 1/2$ inches wide. Lightly coat your hands with flour (the dough will be sticky) and gently press down to flatten the logs.

Place each log on one of the prepared baking sheets. Place in the oven and bake for about 30 minutes, or until golden brown and the center feels soft when touched.

Remove from the oven and transfer the logs to wire racks to cool slightly. Do not remove the silicone mats from the baking sheets.

Lower the oven temperature to 300ºF.

When cool enough to handle, using a serrated knife, cut the logs, crosswise, into slices between $1/4$ inch and $1/2$ inch thick.

Lay the slices, cut-side down, on the baking sheets and place in the oven for about 15 minutes, or until golden brown and crisp.

Remove from the oven and, using a metal spatula, transfer the biscotti to wire racks to cool.

Store, airtight, at room temperature for up to a week.

# Chocolate-Hazelnut Biscotti

This is another traditional biscotti recipe with the classic combination of chocolate and hazelnuts. (This is also the flavor of Nutella, the Italian answer to peanut butter.) If you want to turn it into a very special treat, dip one end into chocolate (see page 93).

**MAKES ABOUT 50 COOKIES**

$5\frac{1}{2}$ cups (1 pound 6 ounces) all-purpose flour

3 cups (1 pound 5 ounces) sugar

$\frac{1}{2}$ cup ($1\frac{3}{4}$ ounces) Dutch-processed cocoa powder

1 tablespoon baking powder

6 large eggs, at room temperature

6 egg yolks, at room temperature

$\frac{1}{3}$ cup honey

$1\frac{1}{2}$ tablespoons pure vanilla extract

1 tablespoon Frangelico or other hazelnut liqueur

1 cup (4 ounces) chopped hazelnuts

Preheat the oven to 350ºF.

Line two baking sheets with nonstick silicone baking mats or parchment paper. (Alternatively, use nonstick baking sheets or lightly butter conventional baking sheets.) Set aside.

Combine the flour, sugar, cocoa, and baking powder in a mixing bowl.

Whisk together the eggs, egg yolks, honey, vanilla, and liqueur in another mixing bowl. When well blended, using a wooden spoon, beat the egg mixture into the dry ingredients. The dough should be very sticky.

Stir in the hazelnuts, mixing until evenly distributed.

Divide the dough into two equal pieces and form each into a log about 10 inches long and $1\frac{1}{2}$ inches wide. Lightly coat your hands with flour (the dough will be sticky) and gently press down to flatten the logs.

Place each log on one of the prepared baking sheets.

Place the pans in the oven and bake for about 30 minutes, or until golden brown.

Remove from the oven and transfer the logs to wire racks to cool slightly. Do not remove the silicone mats from the baking sheets.

Lower the oven temperature to 300ºF.

When cool enough to handle, using a serrated knife, cut the logs, crosswise, into slices between $\frac{1}{4}$ inch and $\frac{1}{2}$ inch thick.

Lay the slices, cut-side down, on the baking sheets and place in the oven for about 15 minutes, or until lightly colored and crisp.

Remove from the oven and using a metal spatula, transfer the biscotti to wire racks to cool.

Store, airtight, at room temperature for up to a week.

# Pistachio Biscotti

These are my favorite biscotti. The cornmeal gives it just the right texture for dunking into a little glass of *vin santo*, a lovely Italian dessert wine. Pistachios and dried apricots make perfect partners.

**MAKES ABOUT 50 COOKIES**

2¾ cups (11 ounces) all-purpose flour

¾ cup (3¾ ounces) polenta

½ tablespoon salt

2 teaspoons baking powder

3 large eggs, at room temperature, plus 1 egg white

2 tablespoons apricot brandy

½ tablespoon pure vanilla extract

¾ cup (6 ounces) unsalted butter, at room temperature

1½ cups (10½ ounces) sugar

2¼ cups (9 ounces) chopped toasted pistachios

1 cup (6 ounces) chopped dried apricots

Preheat the oven to 350°F.

Line two baking sheets with nonstick silicone baking mats or parchment paper. (Alternatively, use nonstick baking sheets or lightly butter conventional baking sheets.) Set aside.

Combine the flour, polenta, salt, and baking powder in a mixing bowl. Set aside.

Whisk together the eggs, brandy, and vanilla together in a mixing bowl. Set aside.

Put the butter in the bowl of a standing electric mixer fitted with the paddle. Begin beating on low speed. Add 1 cup of the sugar, increase the speed to medium, and beat for about 4 minutes, or until light and fluffy.

Add the egg mixture, beating to incorporate.

When combined, add the dry ingredients and beat until well incorporated. When the dough is well-blended, remove the bowl from the mixer and scrape the paddle clean.

Using a wooden spoon, stir in the pistachios and apricots, mixing until evenly distributed. You can also do this in the mixer, but heavy mixing tends to break up the nuts and mash the apricots.

Divide the dough into two equal pieces and form each into a log about 10 inches long and 1½ inches wide. Lightly coat your hands with flour (the dough will be sticky) and gently press down to flatten the logs.

Place each log on one of the prepared baking sheets.

Put the egg white in a small bowl and whisk. Using a pastry brush, lightly coat the top of each log with the egg white. Sprinkle with the remaining ½ cup sugar.

Place the pans in the oven and bake for about 30 minutes, or until golden brown.

Remove from the oven and transfer the logs to wire racks to cool slightly. Do not remove the silicone mats from the baking sheets.

Lower the oven temperature to 300ºF.

When cool enough to handle, using a serrated knife, cut the logs, crosswise, into slices between ¼ inch and ½ inch thick.

Lay the slices, cut-side down, on the baking sheets and place in the oven for about 15 minutes, or until golden brown and crisp.

Remove from the oven and, using a metal spatula, transfer the biscotti to wire racks to cool.

Store, airtight, at room temperature for up to a week.

# Anise Biscotti

Anise is the most traditional flavoring for Italian biscotti. This dough will be sticky and you will need to flour your hands to work with it successfully.

**MAKES ABOUT 50 COOKIES**

2 cups (8 ounces) all-purpose flour

$1\frac{1}{2}$ cups ($10\frac{1}{2}$ ounces) sugar

$\frac{1}{2}$ teaspoon baking powder

$\frac{1}{2}$ teaspoon salt

2 large eggs, at room temperature, plus 1 egg yolk

$1\frac{1}{2}$ tablespoons anisette liqueur, plus more as needed

$1\frac{1}{2}$ tablespoons pure vanilla extract

1 cup ($5\frac{1}{2}$ ounces) whole almonds, skin on

$1\frac{1}{2}$ tablespoons crushed anise seeds

Preheat the oven to 350ºF.

Line two baking sheets with nonstick silicone baking mats or parchment paper. (Alternatively, use nonstick baking sheets or lightly butter conventional baking sheets.) Set aside.

Combine the flour, sugar, baking powder, and salt in a mixing bowl.

Whisk together the eggs, egg yolk, anisette, and vanilla in a mixing bowl. When well-blended, using a wooden spoon, beat the egg mixture into the dry ingredients. The dough should be very sticky. If it is not, add more anisette, a bit at a time.

Stir in the almonds and anise seeds, mixing until evenly distributed.

Divide the dough into two equal pieces and form each into a log about 10 inches long and $1\frac{1}{2}$ inches wide. Lightly coat your hands with flour (the dough will be sticky) and gently press down to flatten the logs.

Place each log on one of the prepared baking sheets.

Place the pans in the oven and bake for about 30 minutes, or until golden brown.

Remove from the oven and transfer the logs to wire racks to cool slightly. Do not remove the silicone mats from the baking sheets.

Lower the oven temperature to 300ºF.

When cool enough to handle, using a serrated knife, cut the logs, crosswise, into slices between $\frac{1}{4}$ inch and $\frac{1}{2}$ inch thick.

Lay the slices, cut-side down, on the baking sheets and place in the oven for about 15 minutes, or until golden brown and crisp.

Remove from the oven and, using a metal spatula, transfer the biscotti to wire racks to cool.

Store, airtight, at room temperature for up to a week.

# Sfogliati 'Crown Pastries'

I remember that my mother was the only one who made sfogliati. They were for communions, confirmations, and baptisms. She may have made them at other times, but I remember the special occasions most. You have to be very careful with these cookies, as they are delicate and fragile. For the perfect presentation, dip them carefully into the honey without breaking the "crown." (I have to say that the little broken pieces always tasted better to me!)

Since sfogliati are an integral part of family celebrations, we always make a big batch. Cut the recipe in half if you don't have a big Italian family to feed!

**MAKES ABOUT 64 COOKIES**

7 cups (1 pound 12 ounces) all-purpose flour, plus more as needed

$^3/_4$ teaspoon salt

$1^3/_4$ cups (14 ounces) vegetable shortening

4 large eggs, at room temperature

$^1/_2$ tablespoon pure vanilla extract

$^1/_2$ cup water, plus more as needed

Vegetable oil for frying (about 2 quarts)

2 cups honey

$^3/_4$ cup ($2^1/_2$ ounces) confectioners' sugar

Combine the 7 cups flour and the salt together on a clean, flat work surface. Add the shortening and, using your fingertips or a pastry blender, work the shortening into the flour until it forms pea-size crumbs. Make a well in the center of the mixture.

Combine the eggs and vanilla in a mixing bowl and whisk to blend completely. Pour the egg mixture into the center of the flour and using your fingertips, work the flour into the eggs. When completely blended, begin adding the $^1/_2$ cup water, working it into the dough. The dough should be soft and tender. If too dry, add more water, 1 tablespoon at a time. If too wet, add about 1 tablespoon flour.

Form the dough into a neat mound and cover with a glass bowl. Let stand for 3 hours.

Lightly flour a clean, flat work surface. Divide the dough into four pieces. Place one-quarter of the dough on the floured surface and, using a rolling pin, roll it out into a 12-by-9-inch rectangle.

Using a pastry wheel or a small sharp knife, cut the dough in half lengthwise then into 24 strips about $4^1/_2$ inches long and $^1/_2$ inch wide.

Working with three strips at a time, braid them together. Form the braid into a circle and press the ends together to seal. Repeat with the second piece of dough.

When all of the pastries have been formed, put the oil in a deep-fat fryer with a basket insert and place over high heat. When the temperature reaches 365°F on a candy thermometer, begin adding the pastries, a few at a time, to the oil. Fry for about 3 minutes, or until golden brown.

Lift the pastries from the oil with a slotted spoon and place on a double layer of paper towels to drain.

While the pastries are cooling, place the honey in small saucepan over low heat to warm up for just a minute or two.

Put the confectioners' sugar in a fine-mesh sieve. Set aside.

Working with one pastry at a time, dip each into the warm honey and immediately sprinkle a bit of confectioners' sugar over the top. Place on a wire rack to set.

Store in layers separated by waxed paper, airtight, at room temperature for up to a day.

# Sfingi

These cookies are a real family favorite that must be eaten as soon as possible after they are fried and drenched in warm honey. Throughout my childhood, sfingi were made for special occasions and holidays and, once in a great while, just because one of the women felt like spending her Sunday afternoon in the kitchen.

**MAKES ABOUT 45 COOKIES**

$2\frac{1}{2}$ cups ($11\frac{1}{4}$ ounces) all-purpose flour

$\frac{1}{2}$ heaping teaspoon baking powder

2 cups water

$\frac{1}{2}$ tablespoon unsalted butter

5 large eggs, at room temperature

Vegetable oil for frying (about 2 quarts)

2 cups honey

Combine the flour and baking powder in a mixing bowl. Set aside.

Combine the water and butter in a medium saucepan over high heat. Bring to a boil and immediately remove from the heat.

Using a wooden spoon, stir the flour mixture into the water in the saucepan, beating until the dough forms a ball. Set aside to cool, about 30 minutes.

When the dough is completely cool, add 2 of the eggs and, using a wooden spoon, beat them into the dough. When completely incorporated, add the remaining eggs, one at a time, beating to incorporate after each addition.

Put the oil in a deep-fat fryer with a basket insert and place over high heat. When the temperature reaches 365°F on a candy thermometer, begin adding pieces of dough, about $\frac{3}{4}$-teaspoonful size, into the oil. The sfingi should spin and bounce around in the oil to cook evenly as they turn golden brown. Do not crowd the pan.

While the sfingi are frying, put the honey in a small saucepan over low heat. Cook, stirring occasionally, just until the honey is warm and has thinned down a bit. Remove from the heat, and keep warm.

Lift the sfingi from the oil with a slotted spoon and place on a double layer of paper towels to drain.

When all of the sfingi are done, place them in a large bowl and pour the warm honey over the top, tossing to coat evenly.

They taste best while still warm, so serve them as quickly as possible.

# Grandma Connie's Light and Fluffy Sfingi

Grandma Connie is my mother's mom. Her sfingi are little dumpling puffs and so, so delicious. She used leftover ricotta (from making her famous lasagna) to give them a light, bouncy texture.

**MAKES ABOUT 60 COOKIES**

$1\frac{1}{2}$ cups (6 ounces) all-purpose flour

1 tablespoon plus $1\frac{1}{2}$ teaspoons baking powder

$\frac{3}{4}$ teaspoon ground cinnamon

2 cups ($1\frac{1}{2}$ pounds) ricotta cheese (see Note)

$\frac{1}{4}$ cup ($1\frac{3}{4}$ ounces) sugar

3 large eggs, at room temperature

Vegetable oil for frying (about 2 quarts)

2 cups honey

Combine the flour, baking powder, and cinnamon in a mixing bowl. Set aside.

Combine the ricotta and sugar in the bowl of a standing electric mixer fitted with the paddle. Beat on medium to blend. Add the eggs, one at a time, beating well after each addition.

When blended, add the dry ingredients and beat for about 3 minutes, or until well incorporated.

Put the oil in a deep-fat fryer with a basket insert and place over high heat. When the temperature reaches 365°F on a candy thermometer, begin adding pieces of dough, about $\frac{3}{4}$-teaspoonful size, into the oil. The sfingi should spin and bounce around in the oil to cook evenly as they turn a dark golden brown. Do not crowd the pan. From time to time, test a sfingi to make sure the center is completely cooked. If the cookies are darkening too quickly, lower the heat and let the oil cool slightly.

While the sfingi are frying, put the honey in a small saucepan over low heat. Cook, stirring occasionally, just until the honey is warm and has thinned down a bit. Remove from the heat, and keep warm.

Lift the sfingi from the hot oil with a slotted spoon, and place on a double layer of paper towels to drain.

When all of the sfingi are done, put them in a large bowl and pour the warm honey over the top, tossing to coat evenly.

They taste best while still warm, so serve them as quickly as possible.

**NOTE:** It is important to use *ricotta impastata* or fresh ricotta. It has a drier curd than the creamy version available in the supermarket dairy section, which is too wet and will make the cookies soggy instead of light and fluffy.

# Grandma Connie's Anise Toast

Grandma Connie always had these cookies on hand—from the freezer, from the oven, from the cookie jar! They are meant to be quite dry with just a hint of anise flavor; perfect for dunking.

If you don't care for anise, you can replace it with 1 teaspoon pure vanilla or pure almond extract.

**MAKES ABOUT 2 DOZEN COOKIES**

$2^1/_2$ cups ($11^1/_4$ ounces) all-purpose flour

$2^1/_2$ teaspoons baking powder

4 large eggs, at room temperature

1 cup (7 ounces) sugar

$^1/_4$ teaspoon anise oil

Preheat the oven to 325ºF.

Line two baking sheets with nonstick silicone baking mats or parchment paper. (Alternatively, use nonstick baking mats or lightly butter conventional baking sheets.) Set aside.

Combine the flour and baking powder in a mixing bowl. Set aside.

Put the eggs in the bowl of a standing electric mixer fitted with the paddle. Beat on low speed. Add the sugar, increase the speed to medium, and beat for 1 minute to blend. Add the oil and beat to incorporate. Add the dry ingredients and beat until fully incorporated.

Lightly coat your hands with flour. Divide the dough into two equal pieces and form each into a log about 10 inches long and 1 inch wide. (The dough will be very loose and sticky.) Using a tablespoon dipped in cool water or flour, lightly press down to flatten each log.

Place each log on one of the prepared baking sheets.

Place the pans in the oven and bake for about 15 minutes, or until light golden brown and dry to the touch. The top should spring back when lightly touched. If it does not spring back, bake for 2 minutes more.

Remove from the oven and using a serrated knife, immediately cut the logs, crosswise, into slices 1 inch thick and 3 inches long. Do not remove the silicone mats from the baking sheets.

Raise the oven temperature to 375ºF.

Lay the slices, cut-side down, on the baking sheets and place in the oven for about 5 minutes, or until golden brown.

Remove from the oven and, using a metal spatula, transfer the cookies to wire racks to cool.

Store, airtight, at room temperature for up to a week.

# Grandma Connie's Wandies

It takes a whole family to make wandies. When I was young, we would all get together at my grandmother's on a December Sunday afternoon just before the holidays to make them. As much as we all loved them, this was the only time of the year when they were made. My mother made one batch of dough and my grandmother made her own batch. One person rolled the dough through the pasta machine, another cut it into strips, two others would be twisting and tying the knots, and the men would be doing the frying. That was how it was done, year after year.

We would always stop in the middle of this monumental chore for a pasta dinner break, but it would be a short one. Then we'd all get right back to our jobs.

At the end of the day, the cookies would be divided among all of the families and taken home in large containers, which would last us through the entire holiday season and be plentiful enough to share with friends and neighbors. My mother's portion was large enough to fill an old-fashioned Charlie Chip potato chip can. Just writing about wandies takes me right back to those warm, wonderful family days.

**MAKES ABOUT 100 COOKIES**

10 cups ($2\frac{1}{2}$ pounds) all-purpose flour

1 tablespoon plus $\frac{1}{2}$ teaspoon baking powder

$\frac{1}{2}$ teaspoon salt

9 large eggs, at room temperature

$2\frac{1}{4}$ cups ($15\frac{3}{4}$ ounces) sugar

$\frac{1}{2}$ cup canola oil

Juice and zest of 2 lemons

$\frac{1}{2}$ tablespoon plus $\frac{1}{2}$ teaspoon pure vanilla extract

1 tablespoon plus 1 teaspoon ground cinnamon

Vegetable oil for frying (about 1 gallon)

Approximately $1\frac{1}{2}$ cups (5 ounces) confectioners' sugar

Sift half of the flour with the baking powder and salt into a mixing bowl. Set aside.

Put the eggs in the bowl of a standing electric mixer fitted with the paddle. Beat on low speed to lighten. Add the sugar, increase the speed to medium, and beat for 3 minutes. Add the canola oil, lemon juice and zest, and vanilla, beating to blend well. When blended, beat in the cinnamon.

Remove the paddle attachment and replace it with the dough hook.

Add the sifted flour mixture and, using the dough hook, knead the dough for about 5 minutes, or until very sticky. Add the remaining flour and continue kneading to incorporate evenly. The dough should be smooth and shiny.

Remove the bowl from the mixer and scrape the paddle clean.

Break off a chunk of the dough, about 8 ounces or any size that fits easily in your pasta machine.

Run the piece of dough through the #2 slot of the pasta machine.

Lay the rolled dough on a clean, flat work surface. Using a pastry wheel or small sharp knife, cut the dough into strips about 2 inches long and 1 inch wide.

Using a small, sharp knife, cut a small slit in the middle of each strip. Bring one end of the dough up and through the slit and shake slightly to make a little curl or, for a different look, tie the dough in a knot.

When all of the cookies are ready, put the oil in a deep-fat fryer with a basket insert and place over high heat. When the temperature reaches 350°F on a candy thermometer, carefully drop the cookies, a few at a time, into the oil. Fry for about 3 minutes, or until golden brown.

Lift the cookies out of the oil with a slotted spoon, and place on a double layer of paper towels to drain.

When all of the cookies are cool, place the confectioners' sugar in a fine-mesh sieve and, tapping the rim gently, sprinkle sugar over the cookies.

Store in layers separated by paper towels, airtight, at room temperature for up to a month.

# Grandma Tina's Chocolate Drop Cookies

These are my ultimate cookie, and my whole family loves them, too. Only Grandma Tina made them, and no matter how many she made, there were never enough to go around. She took her time to ice them perfectly and the walnut decoration had to be just the right size and placed just so.

This is probably the first recipe I made on my own. I still love to make these cookies and I think of her every time I do.

**MAKES ABOUT 4 DOZEN COOKIES**

$2\frac{1}{2}$ ounces unsweetened chocolate

2 cups (8 ounces) all-purpose flour

1 teaspoon baking soda

$\frac{1}{4}$ cup (2 ounces) vegetable shortening

1 cup (7 ounces) dark brown sugar

1 large egg, at room temperature

$\frac{1}{4}$ cup milk

1 teaspoon pure vanilla extract

Chocolate Frosting (page 128)

48 small walnut pieces

Preheat the oven to 350°F.

Line two baking sheets with nonstick silicone baking mats or parchment paper. (Alternatively, use nonstick baking mats or lightly butter conventional baking sheets.) Set aside.

Put the chocolate in the top of a double boiler over simmering water and stir frequently for about 4 minutes, or until the chocolate has melted. Remove from the heat and set aside.

Combine the flour and baking soda in a mixing bowl. Set aside.

Put the shortening in the bowl of a standing electric mixer fitted with the paddle. Begin beating on low speed to soften. Add the brown sugar, increase the speed to medium, and continue to beat for 2 minutes. Add the egg, milk, and vanilla, beating to incorporate.

Reduce the speed to low and add the melted chocolate, beating to incorporate.

Gradually add the flour mixture and beat to just blend, then remove the bowl from the mixer and scrape the paddle clean.

Drop the dough by the heaping tablespoonful, about 2 inches apart, onto the prepared baking sheets. If desired, dampen your fingertip and round off the edges slightly to give a neater finish to the baked cookies.

Place in the oven and bake for about 10 minutes, or just until the center is set. Do not overbake or the cookies will be dry and harden very quickly.

Remove from the oven and, using a metal spatula, transfer the cookies to wire racks to cool.

When cool, lightly coat the top of each cookie with the frosting and place a walnut piece in the center. Return the cookies to the wire racks as they are frosted for about 15 minutes, or until the frosting has set.

Store in layers separated by waxed paper, airtight, at room temperature for up to a week.

# Chocolate Frosting

2 ounces unsweetened chocolate

2 teaspoons unsalted butter, cut into small pieces, at room temperature

1 tablespoon strong coffee, plus more if needed

1 cup (3½ ounces) confectioners' sugar, sifted

Put the chocolate in the top of a double boiler over simmering water. Heat, stirring frequently, for about 4 minutes, or until the chocolate has melted. Remove from the heat. Begin adding bits of butter, beating until the chocolate is smooth and shiny, and quickly whisk in the 1 tablespoon coffee.

Put the confectioners' sugar in a mixing bowl. Using a wooden spoon, stir the melted chocolate mixture into the sugar, beating until glossy. If the frosting is too thick, add more coffee, a bit at a time, to reach spreading consistency.

Use immediately.

# Grandma Tina's Sweet Dough Cookies

My grandmother always combined grape jam, apples, and walnuts with a little sprinkle of cinnamon-sugar when she made these cookies. I have tried many variations—they may be filled with almost anything you like, but this version remains my favorite.

**MAKES ABOUT 4 DOZEN COOKIES**

4 cups (1 pound) all-purpose flour

1 teaspoon baking powder

1 cup (8 ounces) vegetable shortening

1 cup (7 ounces) granulated sugar

4 large eggs, at room temperature

$\frac{1}{4}$ cup milk

FILLING

2 tablespoons light brown sugar

1 tablespoon ground cinnamon

$\frac{1}{2}$ cup (4 ounces) grape jam

1 tart apple, peeled, cored, and cut into $\frac{1}{2}$-inch cubes

$\frac{1}{2}$ cup (2 ounces) chopped walnuts

Preheat the oven to 350ºF.

Line two baking mats with nonstick silicone baking mats or parchment paper. (Alternatively, use nonstick baking sheets or lightly butter conventional baking sheets.) Set aside.

Combine the flour and baking powder in a mixing bowl. Set aside.

Combine the shortening and granulated sugar in the bowl of a standing electric mixer fitted with the paddle. Begin beating on low speed to blend together. Increase the speed to medium and beat for about 3 minutes, or until light and creamy.

Add the eggs, one at a time, and beat to incorporate. When blended, slowly beat in the milk.

Gradually add the dry mixture, beating on low speed until the dough is very shiny, then remove the bowl from the mixer and scrape the paddle clean.

Divide the dough into four equal pieces.

Lightly flour a clean, flat work surface. Working with one piece at a time, use a rolling pin to roll the dough out into a large rectangle $\frac{1}{2}$ inch thick.

**CONT'D**

To make the filling: Combine the brown sugar and cinnamon in a small bowl. Set aside.

Using an offset spatula, spread jam on a dough rectangle, leaving a $\frac{1}{4}$-inch border uncovered around the outside edges. Sprinkle on a little of the cinnamon-sugar (reserve some for sprinkling on top before baking), then spread on an equal amount of apples and walnuts.

Roll up each piece of dough, cigar fashion, to form a neat, tight roll, and place, seam-side down, on a prepared baking sheet.

Sprinkle the top with the remaining cinnamon-sugar.

Repeat to form the other rolls.

Place in the oven and bake for about 15 minutes, or until the tops are a light golden brown.

Remove from the oven and set aside to cool for 30 minutes.

When cool, use a serrated knife to cut each roll, crosswise, into pieces about $\frac{1}{2}$ inch thick. The filling should be slightly swirled in the center.

Store in layers separated by waxed paper, airtight, at room temperature for up to a week.

# Viscotti or Aunt Rose's Famous "S" Cookies

This recipe was passed down from my paternal great-grandmother to her daughters-in-law so they could make them for their husbands exactly the same way she had. One of the husbands was my grandfather. My uncle loved them so much that Aunt Rose went the whole nine yards and baked a batch for him daily. This is why, after years and years of practice, her recipe is the best.

**MAKES 2 DOZEN COOKIES**

$3\frac{1}{2}$ cups (13 ounces) all-purpose flour

4 teaspoons baking powder

$1\frac{1}{2}$ teaspoons ground cinnamon

$\frac{1}{4}$ teaspoon salt

1 cup (7 ounces) granulated sugar

6 tablespoons (3 ounces) vegetable shortening

4 large eggs, at room temperature

$\frac{1}{4}$ cup milk

Approximately $\frac{1}{2}$ cup ($1\frac{3}{4}$ ounces) confectioners' sugar

Preheat the oven to 350°F.

Line two baking sheets with nonstick silicone baking mats or parchment paper. (Alternatively, use nonstick baking sheets or lightly butter conventional baking sheets.) Set aside.

Combine the flour, baking powder, cinnamon, and salt in a mixing bowl. Set aside.

Combine the granulated sugar and shortening in the bowl of a standing electric mixer fitted with the paddle. Begin beating on low speed to blend together. Increase the speed to medium and beat for about 3 minutes, or until light and creamy.

Add the eggs, one at a time, and beat to incorporate. Then beat in the milk. When blended, slowly beat in the reserved dry mixture. When dough is just blended, remove the bowl from the mixer and scrape the paddle clean.

Divide the dough into 24 equal pieces. Using your palms, gently roll each piece into a 3-inch log and then form the log into an "S" shape. Take care to not over-work the dough as this will make the cookies dry and tough. The logs can be formed with your fingertips; they don't have to be smooth and perfectly shaped. They will look just fine after baking. As you shape them, place each cookie on the prepared baking sheets.

Place in the oven and bake for about 10 minutes, or until lightly browned around the edges and the cookie is firm but still feels soft to the touch.

Remove from the oven and, using a metal spatula, transfer the cookies to wire racks to cool slightly.

While the cookies are still warm, place the confectioners' sugar in a fine-mesh sieve and, tapping the rim gently, sprinkle sugar over the cookies.

Serve immediately or let cool completely.

Store in layers separated by waxed paper, airtight, at room temperature for up to a week.

# Aunt Annie's Sesame Seed Cookies

Although many bakers in my family made these, there was something special about Aunt Annie's sesame cookies. They just tasted better than anyone else's. She was so well known for them that she always had them in the house. I remember that whenever I visited, she had a jarful handy for guests who dropped by.

**MAKES ABOUT 4 DOZEN COOKIES**

2 large eggs, at room temperature

1 cup (7 ounces) sugar

$\frac{1}{4}$ cup milk

1 teaspoon pure vanilla extract

2 teaspoons baking powder

1 teaspoon baking soda

4 cups (1 pound) all-purpose flour, sifted

$\frac{1}{4}$ teaspoon salt

1 cup (8 ounces) vegetable shortening

2 cups (12 ounces) sesame seeds

Preheat the oven to 375°F.

Line two baking sheets with nonstick silicone baking mats or parchment paper. (Alternatively, use nonstick baking sheets or lightly butter conventional baking sheets.) Set aside.

Combine the eggs and sugar in a mixing bowl. In another bowl, combine the milk and vanilla with the baking powder and baking soda.

Put the flour and salt in the bowl of a standing electric mixer fitted with the paddle. Add the shortening and begin mixing on low speed to work it into the dry ingredients. Alternate adding the egg mixture and milk mixture in two parts into the flour mixture, beating on low speed after each addition until completely incorporated.

Divide the dough into four equal pieces and form each into a long log about $\frac{1}{2}$ inch in diameter.

Place the sesame seeds on a clean, flat work surface. Roll each log in the sesame seeds to cover generously. Using a serrated knife, cut each log into cookies about 2 inches long and place the cookies, about 1 inch apart, on the prepared baking sheets.

Place them in the oven and bake for about 10 minutes, or until golden brown.

Remove from the oven and, using a metal spatula, transfer the cookies to wire racks to cool.

Store, airtight, at room temperature for up to a week.

# Aunt Fran's Asian Noodle Cookies

My Aunt Fran is the only person I know who makes these no-bake cookies. I think she must have gotten the recipe from a friend or maybe from the back of a box. They certainly aren't a traditional Italian cookie, but they are one of my family's favorites. They are always the first to disappear from a holiday cookie platter.

**MAKES ABOUT 2 DOZEN COOKIES**

One 5-ounce package crispy Chinese chow mein noodles

1 cup (4 ounces) chopped cashew nuts

1 cup (4 ounces) chopped walnuts

2 cups (12 ounces) semisweet chocolate chips

1 cup (6 ounces) butterscotch chips

Line two baking sheets with nonstick silicone baking mats or parchment paper. (Alternatively, use nonstick baking sheets.) Set aside.

Combine the noodles, cashews, and walnuts in a mixing bowl.

Combine the chocolate chips and butterscotch chips in the top of a double boiler over simmering water. Heat, stirring frequently, for about 5 minutes, or until the chips are melted and have blended together. Remove from the heat and pour over the noodle mixture. Stir carefully with a wooden spoon, without breaking up the noodles too much, until the ingredients are coated completely.

Drop the mixture by the teaspoonful onto the prepared baking sheets. Place in the refrigerator for about 30 minutes, or until set.

Store in layers separated by waxed paper, airtight, at room temperature for up to a week.

# Aunt Fran's Clark Bar Cookies

These are Aunt Fran's version of a crunchy truffle. It's more like a candy bar than a cookie, but I still add them to holiday cookie trays.

**MAKES ABOUT 2 DOZEN COOKIES**

3 cups (9 ounces) crispy rice cereal

One 1-pound box confectioners' sugar

One 16-ounce jar smooth peanut butter

$1/2$ cup (4 ounces) unsalted butter, at room temperature

1 pound couverture chocolate (see Note, page 93)

2 tablespoons vegetable oil

Line two baking sheets with nonstick silicone baking mats or parchment paper. (Alternatively, use nonstick baking sheets.) Set aside.

Put the cereal in a large bowl. Add the confectioners' sugar and toss to combine. Add the peanut butter and butter and stir until completely blended.

Using your hands, form the mixture into balls about $3/4$ inch in diameter.

Heat the chocolate in the top of a double boiler over simmering water. When melted, remove from the heat and stir in the vegetable oil.

Using a dipping fork or two kitchen forks, turn the peanut butter balls around in the chocolate to coat completely. Place on the prepared baking sheets to set.

When set, store in layers separated by waxed paper, at room temperature for up to a week.

# Bride's Cookies

My grandmother always made these cookies for weddings, but she also made them for baptisms, communions, and confirmations. (The name "bride's cookies" might come from their white color.) She substituted chocolate chips for the dates whenever she made them for the children.

It is essential to chill the walnuts and dates so the cookies will hold their shape. If your kitchen is warm, keep the batter in the refrigerator as you make the cookies.

**MAKES ABOUT 60 COOKIES**

**4 egg whites, at room temperature**

**One 1-pound box confectioners' sugar, sifted**

**4 cups (1 pound) chopped walnuts, chilled**

**3 cups (1 pound) chopped dates, chilled**

Preheat the oven to 400°F.

Line two baking sheets with nonstick silicone baking mats or parchment paper. (Alternatively, use nonstick baking sheets or lightly butter conventional baking sheets.) Set aside.

Put the egg whites in the bowl of a standing electric mixer fitted with the whip. Beat on high speed for about 4 minutes, or until the whites begin to foam. Add the confectioners' sugar gradually and beat until stiff peaks form. Remove the bowl from the mixer and scrape the paddle clean.

Fold the chilled walnuts and dates into the dough.

Drop the batter by the heaping teaspoonful, about 1 inch apart, onto the prepared baking sheets, taking care that the batter forms a little peak in the center.

Place in the oven and bake for about 4 minutes, or until just barely golden and a bit crisp around the edges. The cookies should be dry on the outside, but still chewy on the interior.

Remove from the oven and, using a metal spatula, *immediately* transfer the cookies to wire racks to cool.

Store in layers separated by waxed paper, airtight, at room temperature for up to a week.

# Wine Cookies

Wine Cookies are the Italian version of cut-out sugar cookies. Since there is absolutely no wine in them, I'm not sure how they got their name—perhaps because they were dunked into sweet wine? There might have been wine in the recipe at one time that eventually got replaced with grape jam. Or maybe because of the rich color they have. I just don't know.

My grandmother always cut them into a variety of shapes and then drizzled confectioners' sugar icing over the top.

**MAKES ABOUT 4 DOZEN COOKIES**

4 cups (1 pound) all-purpose flour, sifted

$3/8$ cup ($1\frac{1}{2}$ ounces) Dutch-processed cocoa powder

$1/4$ cup ($1\frac{3}{4}$ ounces) sugar

1 tablespoon plus 1 teaspoon baking powder

2 teaspoons finely grated orange zest

1 teaspoon ground allspice

$1/2$ teaspoon ground cinnamon

2 large eggs, at room temperature

$1/2$ cup vegetable oil

$1/4$ cup (4 ounces) grape jam

$1/2$ cup (2 ounces) finely chopped walnuts

Preheat the oven to 400°F.

Line two baking sheets with nonstick silicone baking mats or parchment paper. (Alternatively, use nonstick baking sheets or lightly butter conventional baking sheets.) Set aside.

Combine the flour, cocoa powder, sugar, baking powder, orange zest, allspice, and cinnamon in a bowl. Set aside.

Put the eggs in the bowl of a standing electric mixer fitted with the paddle and beat on low speed for 2 minutes. Add the oil and jam and beat to blend.

Remove the paddle attachment and replace it with the dough hook.

Add the reserved flour mixture and knead the dough for about 10 minutes, or until very shiny. Add the walnuts and continue kneading to incorporate evenly. When the dough is shiny, remove the bowl from the mixer and scrape the paddle clean.

Lightly flour a clean, flat work surface and use a rolling pin to roll the dough out into a large rectangle about $1/4$ inch thick.

Cut the dough into diamond shapes using a cookie cutter or by cutting freehand with a small, sharp knife or pastry cutter.

As you cut them, place the cookies about 1 inch apart, on the prepared baking sheets.

Place in the oven and bake for about 10 minutes, or until golden brown.

Remove from the oven and, using a metal spatula, transfer the cookies to wire racks to cool.

Store, airtight or covered in plastic wrap, at room temperature for up to a week. They can also be frozen for up to a month.

# Almond Horns

Although they're called "horns," these cookies are shaped more like a horseshoe. They can be piped into any shape, however, such as the familiar rosette with a little piece of maraschino cherry in the center. The almond paste and egg white combination gives them a wonderful chewy texture.

**MAKES ABOUT 2 DOZEN COOKIES**

$3^1/_2$ cups (13 ounces) all-purpose flour

$^3/_4$ cup (3 ounces) cornstarch

$^1/_2$ tablespoon ground cardamom

$1^1/_4$ cups (10 ounces) unsalted butter, at room temperature

$^1/_2$ cup (3 ounces) almond paste

1 cup (7 ounces) granulated sugar

1 cup ($3^1/_2$ ounces) confectioners' sugar

2 egg whites, at room temperature

1 teaspoon pure vanilla extract

1 cup (4 ounces) sliced almonds

Preheat the oven to 350ºF.

Line two baking sheets with nonstick silicone baking mats or parchment paper. (Alternatively, use nonstick baking sheets or lightly butter conventional baking sheets.) Set aside.

Combine the flour, cornstarch, and cardamom in a mixing bowl. Set aside.

Combine the butter and almond paste in the bowl of a standing electric mixer fitted with the paddle. Beat on low speed to just blend. Increase the speed to medium and beat for about 2 minutes, or until completely blended.

Add the granulated and confectioners' sugars and continue to beat for about 3 minutes, or until light and fluffy.

Reduce the speed and add the egg whites, one at a time, and beat to incorporate, scraping down the sides of the bowl with a rubber spatula after each addition. This must be done slowly so that the almond paste does not become lumpy. Beat in the vanilla until blended, then slowly beat in the dry ingredients. When the dough is just blended, remove the bowl from the mixer and scrape the paddle clean.

Transfer the dough to a pastry bag fitted with the #5 tip. Pipe out U-shaped cookies on the prepared baking sheets, and sprinkle the tops with the almonds.

Place in the oven and bake for about 10 minutes, or until lightly browned and moist in the center.

Remove from the oven and, using a metal spatula, transfer the cookies to wire racks to cool.

Store in layers separated by waxed paper, airtight, at room temperature for up to a week.

# Ciambelli

You can find ciambelli in every Italian bakery, so very few people still make them at home. They can be flavored with citrus or chocolate. Hard on the interior with a sweet, crunchy sugar coating, these are the classic Italian dunking cookies.

**MAKES ABOUT 4 DOZEN COOKIES**

1 cup (8 ounces) vegetable shortening

3 cups (12 ounces) all-purpose flour

2 tablespoons baking powder

6 large eggs, at room temperature

1 cup (7 ounces) granulated sugar

Juice and zest of 1 orange

1 teaspoon pure vanilla extract

Approximately 3 cups (10½ ounces) confectioners' sugar

Put the shortening in a small saucepan over low heat. Heat just until it melts. Remove from the heat and allow to cool.

Preheat the oven to 375°F.

Line two baking sheets with nonstick silicone baking mats or parchment paper. (Alternatively, use nonstick baking sheets or lightly butter conventional baking sheets.) Set aside.

Combine the flour and baking powder in a mixing bowl. Set aside.

Combine the eggs and granulated sugar in the bowl of a standing electric mixer fitted with the paddle. Beat on low speed to just combine; then increase the speed to medium and beat for about 10 minutes, or until very light and fluffy.

Add the orange juice and zest along with the vanilla and beat to blend, then beat in the cooled, melted shortening.

Gradually add the flour mixture, beating to incorporate. When the dough is well blended, remove the bowl from the mixer and scrape the paddle clean.

Place the confectioners' sugar in a large, shallow container.

Using about a teaspoon of dough, form balls and roll each in the confectioners' sugar.

Place the cookies, about 1 inch apart, on the prepared baking sheets.

Place in the oven and bake for about 10 minutes, or until golden brown.

Remove from the oven and, using a metal spatula, transfer the cookies to wire racks to cool.

Store in layers separated by waxed paper, airtight, at room temperature for up to a week.

# Pinulata

These are my mom's favorite cookies. They are a sure sign of Christmas and Easter, and they are always on the table during these holidays. She learned how to make them from her mother and I would guess that it had been passed down through several generations of Italian mothers before her. She shaped them into either a wreath or a cross. They can also be made into tree shapes and other Christmas ornaments.

It's important to do the shaping while the honey is still warm. As it cools, the dough gets too stiff to work with. I remember my mom working so quickly to finish making the perfect shapes that she often burned her fingers. Without the nuts, these cookies are called struffoli.

### MAKES ABOUT 5 WREATHS

$3\frac{1}{2}$ cups (14 ounces) chopped walnuts

2 cups (8 ounces) chopped hazelnuts

2 cups (8 ounces) chopped almonds

4 large eggs, at room temperature

$3\frac{1}{2}$ cups (15 ounces) all-purpose flour

$\frac{1}{4}$ teaspoon salt

4 cups vegetable oil

2 cups honey

$\frac{2}{3}$ cup ($4\frac{1}{2}$ ounces) sugar

2 tablespoons water

1 teaspoon ground cinnamon

Preheat the oven to 300°F.

Combine the nuts in a large baking pan, taking care that they are in one layer. Place in the oven and bake for about 8 minutes, or just until lightly toasted. Watch them carefully as nuts can burn very quickly.

Remove from the oven and let cool.

Put the eggs in a small bowl and, using a whisk, beat well.

Sift together the flour and salt into a neat pile on a clean, flat work surface. Make a well in the center of the flour. Pour about one-quarter of the beaten eggs into the well and begin kneading them into the flour. Continue adding eggs, one-quarter at a time, and kneading until it forms a firm dough. Shape the dough into a smooth ball.

Place the ball on a clean surface, cover with a glass bowl, and let rest for at least 2 hours or up to 5 hours.

Divide the dough into four equal pieces. Working with one piece at a time, form it into a neat log about $\frac{1}{4}$ inch in diameter. Cut each log into small, almond-size pieces.

Put the oil in a deep-fat fryer with a basket insert and place over high heat. When the oil has reached 350°F on a candy thermometer, drop the dough pieces into the oil. Fry for about 3 minutes, or until golden brown.

Lift the cookies out of the oil with a slotted spoon and place on a double layer of paper towels to drain.

Combine the honey, sugar, 2 tablespoons water, and cinnamon in a large heavy-bottomed saucepan over medium heat. Bring to a boil and boil for 10 minutes. Lower the heat and keep at a bare simmer. Add the drained balls and the nuts to the honey mixture, stirring to distribute the syrup throughout and to coat them evenly.

Lightly wipe a clean, flat work surface with cool water. Pour about one-quarter of the honey mixture onto the damp surface. Wetting your hands to prevent getting burned, shape the mixture into any form you desire. Continue shaping the remaining honey mixture in the same way.

Store in layers separated by waxed paper, airtight, at room temperature for up to a week.

To eat, cut the shapes up into bite-size pieces.

# CHAPTER 8

# BROWNIES AND BARS

# Milk & Cookies Bakery Celestial Brownies

These are the brownies that have been named New York City's best time and again. They are rich and fudgy; the secret is in the flour/egg ratio. The use of bittersweet or even extra-bitter chocolate helps to offset the sweetness. Because these brownies require a deep chocolate flavor, using a top-quality chocolate is of the utmost importance.

**MAKES ONE 17¼-BY-11½-BY-1-INCH PAN**

1½ pounds bittersweet chocolate, chopped into chunks

1 cup plus 1½ tablespoons (9 ounces) unsalted butter, at room temperature

5 large eggs, at room temperature

1½ cups (10½ ounces) sugar

½ tablespoon pure vanilla extract

¾ cup (3¼ ounces) all-purpose flour, sifted

Preheat the oven to 350°F.

Lightly coat a large jelly-roll pan with nonstick vegetable spray. Lay a piece of parchment paper in the pan, taking care that it fits neatly at the sides and corners. Set aside.

Combine the chocolate with the butter in the top of a double boiler over simmering water. Heat, stirring frequently, for about 5 minutes, or until the chocolate and butter have melted and blended together. Remove from the heat and set aside.

Put the eggs in the bowl of a standing electric mixer fitted with the whisk. Beat on low speed to combine. Increase the speed and beat for 1 minute. With the motor running, slowly add the sugar and beat until the mixture forms a soft ribbon when lifted from the bowl with a spoon.

Reduce the speed to medium and, with the motor running, beat in the chocolate mixture along with the vanilla to combine.

Add the flour and beat just to combine.

Scrape the batter into the prepared pan and place in the oven. Bake for about 30 minutes, or until the edges begin to pull away from the sides of the pan and a cake tester inserted into the center comes out clean.

Remove from the oven and set the pan on a wire rack to cool.

When cool, use a serrated knife to cut the brownies into 2½-inch squares.

Store, airtight, at room temperature for up to a week.

# Kahlúa Brownies

I absolutely love the flavor of strong coffee and deep, dark chocolate. This brownie combines both of these flavors with the added sweetness of coffee liqueur. It's definitely for the R-rated crowd!

**MAKES ONE 17¼-BY-11½-BY-1-INCH PAN**

$4\frac{2}{3}$ cups (1 pound 12 ounces) semisweet chocolate chips

6 ounces bittersweet chocolate, chopped into chunks

2 cups (1 pound) unsalted butter, at room temperature

$1\frac{1}{4}$ cups (5 ounces) all-purpose flour, sifted

1 tablespoon baking powder

1 teaspoon salt

6 large eggs, at room temperature

$2\frac{1}{4}$ cups (15¾ ounces) granulated sugar

¼ cup Kahlúa or other coffee liqueur

3 tablespoons instant espresso powder

2 tablespoons pure vanilla extract

2 tablespoons vodka

3 cups (12 ounces) walnut pieces or pecan halves

GLAZE

$1\frac{1}{4}$ cups (4¼ ounces) confectioners' sugar, sifted

3 tablespoons Kahlúa or other coffee liqueur

Combine $2\frac{2}{3}$ cups of the chocolate chips with the bittersweet chocolate and butter in the top of a double boiler over simmering water. Heat, stirring frequently, for about 5 minutes, or until the chocolate and butter have melted and blended together. Remove from the heat and set aside to cool slightly.

Combine 1 cup of the flour with the baking powder and salt in a medium mixing bowl. Set aside.

Put the eggs in another medium mixing bowl and, using a wooden spoon, stir in the granulated sugar, Kahlúa, espresso powder, vanilla, and vodka until well blended.

When the egg mixture is blended, stir in the still-warm chocolate mixture to combine. Set aside to cool.

Preheat the oven to 350°F.

Lightly coat a 17¼-by-11½-by-1-inch jelly-roll pan with nonstick vegetable spray. Lay a piece of parchment paper in the pan, taking care that it fits neatly at the sides and corners. Set aside.

Combine the walnuts with the remaining 2 cups chocolate chips and ¼ cup flour in a mixing bowl. Toss to coat the nuts and chips with the flour. Set aside.

When the chocolate mixture is cool, stir in the baking powder mixture. When blended, add the nut/chocolate/flour mixture, and beat to just combine.

Scrape the batter into the prepared pan and place in the oven. Bake for 15 minutes and then turn the pan to ensure even baking. Reduce the oven temperature to 325ºF and continue to bake for 15 minutes, or until the edges begin to pull away from the sides of the pan and a cake tester inserted into the center comes out clean.

Remove from the oven and set the pan on a wire rack to cool completely.

To make the glaze: Combine the confectioners' sugar and Kahlúa in a small mixing bowl, beating with a wooden spoon until smooth.

Use an offset spatula to lightly coat the top of the cooled brownies with the glaze. Let rest for about 15 minutes, or until the glaze has set.

When set, use a serrated knife to cut the brownies into large squares.

Store in layers separated by waxed paper, airtight, at room temperature for up to a week.

# White Chocolate-Hazelnut Brownies

This is my version of the blondie, a lighter and often denser brownie. The white chocolate keeps the bar moist and chewy. I prefer hazelnuts with the white chocolate, but you can use any nut you like.

**MAKES ONE 17¼-BY-11½-BY-1-INCH PAN**

1 pound plus 2 ounces white chocolate, chopped

1 cup plus 2 tablespoons (9 ounces) unsalted butter, at room temperature

3¾ cups (14 ounces) all-purpose flour, sifted

¾ teaspoon baking powder

¾ teaspoon salt

6 large eggs, at room temperature

2½ cups plus 1½ tablespoons (18 ounces) sugar

1 tablespoon pure vanilla extract

1⅓ cups (8 ounces) semisweet chocolate chips

1½ cups (6 ounces) chopped toasted hazelnuts

GLAZE

1 pound white chocolate, chopped

1 cup heavy cream

Combine the white chocolate and butter in the top of a double boiler over simmering water. Heat, stirring frequently, for about 5 minutes, or until the chocolate and butter have melted and blended together. Remove from the heat and set aside to cool.

Preheat the oven to 325°F.

Lightly coat a 17¼-by-11½-by-1-inch jelly-roll pan with nonstick vegetable spray. Lay a piece of parchment paper in the pan, taking care that it fits neatly at the sides and corners. Set aside.

Combine the flour, baking powder, and salt in a medium mixing bowl. Set aside.

Put the eggs in the bowl of a standing electric mixer fitted with the paddle. Beat on low speed to just combine, then increase the speed and beat until light and frothy. Add the sugar and beat until well incorporated. Add the cooled chocolate mixture and vanilla and beat to blend, then beat in the reserved flour mixture. Remove the bowl from the mixer and scrape the paddle clean.

Using a wooden spoon, stir in the chocolate chips and hazelnuts, beating until evenly distributed. You can also do this in the mixer, but heavy mixing tends to break up the chocolate and nuts and the result is a less chunky brownie.

Scrape the batter into the prepared pan and place in the oven. Bake for 15 minutes, then turn the pan to ensure even baking. Reduce the oven temperature to 325°F and continue to bake for 15 minutes, or until the edges begin to pull away from the sides of the pan and a cake tester inserted into the center comes out clean.

Remove from the oven and set the pan on a wire rack to cool completely.

To make the glaze: Place the white chocolate in a heatproof bowl.

Put the cream in a small saucepan over medium-low heat and cook just until bubbles form around the edge. Immediately remove from the heat and pour over the chocolate. Let stand for about 4 minutes; then, using a whisk, very slowly stir the chocolate out from the center of the bowl so the chocolate and cream combine and have a smooth texture, without air bubbles.

When smooth, pour the glaze over the cooled brownies and use an offset spatula to spread it in a thin, even layer. Let rest for about 30 minutes, or until the glaze has set.

Use a serrated knife to cut the brownies into large squares.

Store in layers separated by waxed paper, airtight, at room temperature for up to a week.

# Another Great Brownie

This is another favorite brownie recipe; it combines two different chocolates and adds a good dose of nuts. Any type of nut will work here, even unsalted peanuts. These are rich, decadent brownies that can be cut into smaller squares as a little goes a long way.

**MAKES ONE 17¼-BY-11½-BY-1-INCH PAN**

$4^2/_3$ cups (1 pound 12 ounces) semisweet chocolate chips

6 ounces bittersweet chocolate, chopped into chunks

2 cups (1 pound) unsalted butter, at room temperature

$1^1/_4$ cups (5 ounces) all-purpose flour, sifted

1 tablespoon baking powder

1 teaspoon salt

6 large eggs, at room temperature

$1^1/_4$ cups ($8^3/_4$ ounces) sugar

3 tablespoons instant espresso powder

2 tablespoons pure vanilla extract

3 cups (12 ounces) nut pieces such as walnuts, pecans, or hazelnuts

Combine $2^2/_3$ cups of the chocolate chips with the bittersweet chocolate and butter in the top of a double boiler over simmering water. Heat, stirring frequently, for about 5 minutes, or until the chocolate and butter have melted and blended together. Remove from the heat and set aside to cool slightly.

Combine 1 cup of the flour with the baking powder and salt in a medium mixing bowl. Set aside.

Put the eggs in another medium mixing bowl and, using a wooden spoon, stir in the sugar, espresso powder, and vanilla until well blended. Do not beat.

When the egg mixture is blended, stir in the still-warm chocolate mixture and set aside to cool.

Preheat the oven to 350°F.

Lightly coat a 17¼-by-11½-by-1-inch jelly-roll pan with nonstick vegetable spray. Lay a piece of parchment paper in the pan, taking care that it fits neatly at the sides and corners. Set aside.

Combine the nuts with the remaining 2 cups chocolate chips and ¼ cup flour in a mixing bowl. Toss to coat the nuts and chips with the flour. Set aside.

When the chocolate mixture is cool, stir in the baking powder mixture to blend. Add the nut/chocolate/flour mixture, and beat to just combine.

Scrape the batter into the prepared pan and place in the oven. Bake for 15 minutes, then turn the pan to ensure even baking. Reduce the oven temperature to 325°F and continue to bake for 15 minutes, or until the edges begin to pull away from the sides of the pan and a cake tester inserted into the center comes out clean.

Remove from the oven and set the pan on a wire rack to cool.

When cool, use a serrated knife to cut the brownies into 2½-inch squares.

Store, airtight, at room temperature for up to a week.

# Crispy Chocolate Chip Bars

These bars are a big hit with children, so much so that I often bake the batter in a 9-inch cake pan and create a decorated cake for kids' parties.

**MAKES ONE 17¼-BY-11½-BY-1-INCH PAN**

2¼ cups (10 ounces) all-purpose flour, sifted

1 teaspoon salt

½ teaspoon baking soda

1 cup (8 ounces) unsalted butter, at room temperature

¾ cup (5 ounces) granulated sugar

¾ cup (5 ounces) light brown sugar

2 large eggs, at room temperature

1 teaspoon pure vanilla extract

2 cups (12 ounces) semisweet chocolate chips

1 cup (4 ounces) chopped walnuts or any other nut


Preheat the oven to 375°F.

Lightly coat a 17¼-by-11½-by-1-inch jelly-roll pan with nonstick vegetable spray. Lay a piece of parchment paper in the pan, taking care that it fits neatly at the sides and corners. Set aside.

Combine the flour, salt, and baking soda in a small bowl. Set aside.

Put the butter in the bowl of a standing electric mixer fitted with the paddle. Begin beating on low speed to soften. Increase the speed to medium and beat for about 3 minutes, or until light and creamy.

With the motor running, gradually add the granulated sugar and then the brown sugar, beating until very light and creamy.

Add the eggs, one at a time, and beat to incorporate. Beat in the vanilla and when blended, slowly beat in the reserved flour mixture. When the dough is well blended, remove the bowl from the mixer and scrape the paddle clean.

Using a wooden spoon, stir in the chocolate chips and nuts, beating until evenly distributed. You can also do this in the mixer, but heavy mixing tends to break up the chocolate and nuts and the result is a less chunky bar.

Scrape the batter into the prepared pan and place in the oven. Bake for 25 minutes, or until the edges begin to pull away from the sides of the pan and a cake tester inserted into the center comes out clean.

Remove from the oven and set the pan on a wire rack to cool.

When cool, use a serrated knife to cut into small bars.

Store in layers separated by waxed paper, airtight, at room temperature for up to a week.

BROWNIES AND BARS  153

# Pecan Bars

Chewy, gooey, crunchy bars with just the right amount of honey flavor! For extra oomph, drizzle the top with melted bittersweet chocolate.

**MAKES ONE 17¼-BY-11½-BY-1-INCH PAN**

Sugar Cookie Base Dough (page 70)

FILLING

1 cup (7 ounces) light brown sugar

½ cup honey

½ cup plus 2 tablespoons (5 ounces) unsalted butter

¼ teaspoon freshly grated lemon zest

¼ teaspoon freshly grated orange zest

2 tablespoons heavy cream, at room temperature

2½ cups (10 ounces) coarsely chopped pecans

Lightly coat a 17¼-by-11½-by-1-inch jelly-roll pan with nonstick vegetable spray. Lay a piece of parchment paper in the pan, taking care that it fits neatly at the sides and corners. Set aside.

Prepare the Sugar Cookie Base Dough.

Lightly flour a clean, flat work surface. Place the dough in the center of the floured surface. Using a rolling pin, roll the dough out to a rectangle about 18 inches by 12 inches and ⅛ inch thick. Carefully place the dough into the prepared pan, gently fitting it up the sides of the pan so it comes all the way to the top edge. Pinch off any excess dough. Place in the refrigerator to chill for 1 hour.

Preheat the oven to 350°F.

Remove the pan from the refrigerator. Cover the dough with a piece of parchment paper cut to fit, then cover the parchment paper with another baking pan that fits inside and will hold the dough down flat as it bakes.

Place in the oven and bake for about 15 minutes, or just until the crust has set but has not taken on any color. Remove the pan and parchment paper covering the dough and continue to bake for 15 minutes, or until golden brown.

Remove from the oven and set on a wire rack to cool. Do not turn off the oven.

To make the filling: Combine the brown sugar and honey with the butter and lemon and orange zests in a medium saucepan over low heat. Cook, stirring constantly, for about 4 minutes, or until the butter has completely melted. Raise the heat to medium and bring to a boil. Boil, stirring constantly, for exactly 3 minutes. Remove from the heat and immediately stir in the cream followed by the pecans.

Pour the hot filling into the crust, spreading it out with a spatula in an even layer.

Place in the oven and bake for 15 minutes, or until the filling has set in the center.

Remove from the oven and set on a wire rack to cool. When cool, transfer to the refrigerator to chill completely.

When cold, remove from the refrigerator and use a serrated knife to cut into small bars.

Store in layers separated by waxed paper, airtight, at room temperature for up to a week.

# Magic Bars

These bars are known by various aliases. I have heard them called Hello, Dollys and Coconut-Butterscotch Meltaways as well as Magic Bars (my preference). Whatever they are called, everyone seems to have had a relative who made them and cut them into bite-size pieces. At Milk & Cookies Bakery, we cut them into big bars—one bite is never enough.

**MAKES ONE 17¼-BY-11½-BY-1-INCH PAN**

3 cups (15 ounces) graham cracker crumbs

2 cups (1 pound) unsalted butter, cut into pieces

One 14-ounce can sweetened condensed milk

2½ cups (1 pound) semisweet chocolate chips

2½ cups (1 pound) butterscotch chips

2 cups (8 ounces) sweetened coconut flakes

Preheat the oven to 350°F.

Put the graham cracker crumbs in a mixing bowl. Set aside.

Put the butter in a medium saucepan over low heat. Cook for about 4 minutes, or just until the butter has completely melted. Immediately pour the melted butter over the graham cracker crumbs and stir until well combined.

Press the graham cracker mixture into the bottom of a 17¼-by-11½-by-1-inch jelly-roll pan, taking care to form an even layer.

Pour the condensed milk over the graham cracker crust, smoothing it out with a spatula.

Spread the chocolate chips in an even layer over the condensed milk, then spread an even layer of butterscotch chips over the chocolate. Sprinkle the coconut evenly over the top.

Place in the oven and bake for about 12 minutes, or until the chocolate and butterscotch chips have melted and the coconut is lightly browned.

Remove from the oven and place the pan on a wire rack to cool.

When cool, use a serrated knife to cut into small bars or 2-inch squares.

Store in layers separated by waxed paper, airtight, at room temperature for up to a week.

# Linzer Bars

This is my version of the classic *Linzertorte* originally created in Linz, Austria. The dough has just the right touch of hazelnut, almond, and cinnamon to complement the raspberry jam and to keep it close to tradition.

**MAKES ONE 17¼-BY-11½-BY-1-INCH PAN**

**3 cups (12 ounces) all-purpose flour**

**1 cup (7 ounces) hazelnut flour**

**½ cup (2½ ounces) almond flour**

**½ teaspoon baking powder**

**½ teaspoon ground cinnamon**

**Pinch of salt**

**2 cups (1 pound) unsalted butter, at room temperature**

**1¼ cups (8¾ ounces) sugar**

**4 large eggs, at room temperature**

**1 cup (10 ounces) good-quality raspberry jam**

**Egg wash (see Note)**

Combine the all-purpose flour with the hazelnut flour, almond flour, baking powder, cinnamon, and salt in a mixing bowl. Set aside.

Put the butter in the bowl of a standing electric mixer fitted with the paddle. Begin beating on low speed to soften. Increase the speed to medium and beat for about 3 minutes, or until light and creamy.

With the motor running, gradually add the sugar, beating until very light and creamy. Add the eggs, one at a time, and beat well to incorporate after each addition.

With the motor running, slowly add the reserved flour mixture and beat until completely blended, then remove the bowl from the mixer and scrape the paddle clean.

Divide the dough in half. Shape each half into a rectangle and cover tightly in plastic wrap. Place in the refrigerator for about 1 hour, or until thoroughly chilled.

Line a 17¼-by-11½-by-1-inch jelly-roll pan with parchment paper. Set aside.

Preheat the oven to 325ºF.

Lightly flour a clean, flat work surface. Remove the dough from the refrigerator and unwrap. Place one piece of dough on the floured surface and, using a rolling pin, roll it into a neat, even rectangle the same size as the pan. Transfer it to the prepared pan and refrigerate for 30 minutes. Roll out the second piece of dough the same way, then use a pastry cutter or small, sharp knife to cut it lengthwise into strips about 1 inch wide.

Remove the chilled dough from the refrigerator and, using an offset spatula, cover the surface with the raspberry jam, smoothing it out in an even layer. Arrange the strips of dough in a lattice pattern, spaced about ¾ inch apart, over the jam, carefully pinching the loose ends into the edges of the bottom crust. Brush strips with egg wash.

Bake for about 25 minutes, or until the dough is golden brown and cooked through.

Remove from the oven and place the pan on a wire rack to cool.

When cool, use a serrated knife to cut into small bars.

Store in a single layer, airtight, at room temperature for up to a week.

**NOTE:** Egg wash is made by vigorously whisking 1 whole egg with 1 tablespoon water, milk, or cream. Brushing it on pastries and other baked goods with a pastry brush before baking produces a golden sheen on the finished crust.

BROWNIES AND BARS  157

# Apple Crumble Bars

These bars run a very close second to the classic American apple pie. However, not only can you use apples in them, you can also try making them with ripe quince or firm pears for variety.

**MAKES ONE 17¼-BY-11½-BY-1-INCH PAN**

2¼ cups (10 ounces) all-purpose flour

½ teaspoon baking powder

½ teaspoon salt

1 cup (8 ounces) unsalted butter, at room temperature

½ cup (3½ ounces) plus 1 tablespoon light brown sugar, lightly packed

1 large egg, at room temperature

1 tablespoon granulated sugar

1 teaspoon ground cinnamon

3 large Granny Smith apples, peeled, cored, and cut into 1-inch cubes

1 tablespoon fresh lemon juice

Cinnamon Crumble (facing page)

Preheat the oven to 350ºF.

Lightly coat a 17¼-by-11½-by-1-inch jelly-roll pan with nonstick vegetable spray. Lay a piece of parchment paper in the pan, taking care that it fits neatly at the sides and corners. Set aside.

Combine the flour, baking powder, and salt in a small bowl. Set aside.

Put the butter in the bowl of a standing electric mixer fitted with the paddle. Begin beating on low speed. Increase the speed to medium and beat for about 3 minutes, or until light and creamy.

With the motor running, gradually add the ½ cup brown sugar, beating until very light and creamy.

Add the egg, beating to incorporate. When blended, slowly beat in the reserved flour mixture. When the dough is well blended, remove the bowl from the mixer and scrape the paddle clean.

Scrape the dough into the prepared pan and, using your hands, carefully press it into a thin, even layer.

Combine the remaining 1 tablespoon brown sugar with the granulated sugar and cinnamon in a small bowl. Set aside.

Place half of the apples in an even layer over the dough. Sprinkle with the lemon juice and then with the cinnamon-sugar. Top with another layer of sliced apples. Sprinkle the crumble over the top in an even layer.

Place in the oven and bake for about 35 minutes, or until the crust is golden, the apples are bubbling, and the crumble is lightly browned.

Remove from the oven and set on a wire rack to cool.

When cool, use a serrated knife to cut into bars.

Store in a single layer, airtight, at room temperature for up to a week.

# Cinnamon Crumble

1 cup (4 ounces) all-purpose flour

$2/3$ cup ($4^1/2$ ounces) light brown sugar

$2/3$ cup ($4^1/2$ ounces) granulated sugar

1 tablespoon plus 1 teaspoon ground cinnamon

$1/2$ cup (4 ounces) unsalted butter, chilled and cut into cubes

Combine the flour with the brown sugar, granulated sugar, and cinnamon in a small mixing bowl. Add the butter and, using your fingertips, work the butter into the dry ingredients until coarse crumbs are formed.

Store, airtight, in the refrigerator for up to 2 weeks or in the freezer for up to a month.

# Toffee Squares

These yummy squares are a cross between a candy bar and a cookie, with cookie dough for the crust and melted chocolate and coconut combined into a candylike topping. They are always a hit.

**MAKES ONE 10-INCH SQUARE PAN**

2 cups (8 ounces) all-purpose flour

¼ teaspoon salt

¼ teaspoon baking soda

⅔ cup (5 ounces) unsalted butter, chilled slightly

2 cups (14 ounces) light brown sugar, firmly packed

2 large eggs, at room temperature

2 teaspoons pure vanilla extract

1¼ cups (5 ounces) chopped peanuts

1½ cups (9 ounces) semisweet chocolate chips

½ cup (3 ounces) butterscotch chips

½ cup (2 ounces) chopped walnuts

½ cup (4 ounces) unsweetened coconut flakes

Preheat the oven to 350°F.

Lightly coat a 10-inch square baking pan with non-stick vegetable spray. Lay a piece of parchment paper in the pan, taking care that it fits neatly at the sides and corners. Set aside.

Combine the flour, salt, and baking soda in a small bowl. Set aside.

Put the butter in the bowl of a standing electric mixer fitted with the paddle. Begin beating on low speed. Increase the speed to medium and beat for about 3 minutes, or until light and creamy.

With the motor running, gradually add the brown sugar, beating until very light and creamy.

Add the eggs, one at a time, beating well after each addition. Add the vanilla and when blended, slowly beat in the reserved flour mixture. While the dough is still streaky, remove the bowl from the mixer and scrape the paddle clean.

Using a wooden spoon, stir in the peanuts and 1 cup of the chocolate chips, beating until evenly distributed.

Scrape the dough into the prepared pan and, using your hands, carefully press it into an even layer.

Sprinkle the remaining ½ cup chocolate chips over the dough, followed by the butterscotch chips, walnuts, and coconut.

Place in the oven and bake for about 30 minutes, or until the cookie crust is golden and the topping is bubbly and lightly browned.

Remove from the oven and set on a wire rack to cool.

When cool, use a serrated knife to cut into small squares.

Store in layers separated by waxed paper, airtight, at room temperature for up to a week.

# Honey-Lavender Shortbread

I happen to love both the fragrance and flavor of fresh lavender. To enjoy these cookies, you really do need to have an appreciation for this pungent herb. Luckily, I find that the honey adds just the right amount of sweetness.

**MAKES ABOUT 30 COOKIES**

**2 cups (9 ounces) all-purpose flour, sifted**

**1 tablespoon edible fresh or dried lavender**

**¾ teaspoon salt**

**½ teaspoon baking powder**

**¾ cup (6 ounces) unsalted butter, at room temperature**

**½ cup (1¾ ounces) confectioners' sugar**

**2 tablespoons honey, preferably lavender**

Combine the flour, lavender, salt, and baking powder in a mixing bowl. Set aside.

Put the butter in the bowl of a standing electric mixer fitted with the paddle. Begin beating on low speed. Add the confectioners' sugar and honey, increase the speed to medium, and beat until light and fluffy.

Add the reserved flour mixture, beating to just combine.

Scrape the dough onto a piece of parchment paper. With the dough close to the edge of the paper, pat it into a smooth, even log. Start rolling up the dough in the parchment paper until it forms a very tight, neat log. Place in the refrigerator for at least 1 hour, or until very firm.

When ready to bake, preheat the oven to 350°F. Line two baking sheets with parchment paper.

Remove the dough from the refrigerator and unwrap. Using a serrated knife, cut the log into ½-inch-thick slices. Place the slices, about 1 inch apart, on the prepared baking sheets.

Place in the oven and bake for about 8 minutes, or until light golden brown. Remove from the oven and transfer the cookies to wire racks to cool.

Store, airtight, at room temperature for up to a week.

# Vanilla Shortbread

Perfect for afternoon tea, these cookies are much like the British classic that is always on the tea tray. Rather than the usual wedge, these get made in a big pan and cut into bars.

**MAKES ONE 17¼-BY-11½-BY-1-INCH PAN**

**1½ pounds (24 ounces) unsalted butter, at room temperature**

**1 cup (7 ounces) sugar, plus more for sprinkling**

**3 cups (12 ounces) all-purpose flour, sifted**

**2 tablespoons pure vanilla extract or 1 tablespoon vanilla paste**

Preheat the oven to 325°F.

Lightly coat a 17¼-by-11½-by-1-inch jelly-roll pan with nonstick vegetable spray. Lay a piece of parchment paper in the pan, taking care that it fits neatly at the sides and corners. Set aside.

Put the butter in the bowl of a standing electric mixer fitted with the paddle. Begin beating on low speed. Increase the speed to medium and beat for about 3 minutes, or until light and creamy.

With the motor running, gradually add the 1 cup sugar, beating until very light and creamy, then slowly beat in the flour. Add the vanilla. When the dough is well blended, remove the bowl from the mixer and scrape the paddle clean.

Scrape the dough into the prepared pan and, using your fingertips, press the dough into a flat, even layer.

Using a kitchen fork, prick the entire surface of the dough and lightly sprinkle it with sugar.

Place in the oven and bake for about 20 minutes, or just until slightly colored and set in the center. Lower the oven to 300°F and continue to bake for 15 minutes, or until nicely colored.

Remove from the oven and place the pan on a wire rack. Let cool for about 10 minutes.

When cool, use a serrated knife to cut the shortbread into small bars. Let cool completely.

Store, airtight, at room temperature for up to a week.

# Crispy Rice Treats

It doesn't seem to matter that these are easy to make and that every child has made them—Crispy Rice Treats are one of the most popular Mi k & Cookies Bakery treats. I think it is partly because they recall fond childhood memories and partly because they are a treat without overindulging.

**MAKES ONE 13-BY-9-BY-3-INCH PAN**

1 cup (8 ounces) unsalted butter, at room temperature

4 pounds marshmallows

5 cups (1½ pounds) crispy rice cereal

Lightly coat a 13-by-9-by-3-inch pan with nonstick vegetable spray. Lay a piece of parchment paper in the pan, taking care that it fits neatly at the sides and corners. Set aside.

Put the butter in a large, heavy-bottomed saucepan over medium heat. Cook, stirring, for about 3 minutes, or until the butter has melted completely.

Add the marshmallows and cook, stirring constantly, for about 7 minutes, or until the marshmallows have melted into the butter. Remove from the heat.

Working quickly, add the cereal to the hot mixture, stirring constantly until the cereal is completely covered in the syrup.

Butter a rubber spatula and scrape the hot mixture into the prepared pan. Using your fingertips, gently press the mixture into an even layer to fill the pan completely.

Set aside to cool. When cool, use a serrated knife or a cookie cutter to cut into the desired shapes.

Store in layers separated by waxed paper, airtight, at room temperature for up to a week.

SOURCES

## Specialty Pastry Supplies: Chocolate, Candy Bits and Pieces, Sanding Sugars, Cookie Decorations

**CK PRODUCTS**
6510 Jimmy Carter Boulevard
Norcross, GA 30071
888.484.2517
www.ckproducts.com

**INSTANT WHIP INC.**
3226 62nd Street
Flushing, NY 11377
718.278.1652
www.instantwhip.com

**KALUSTYAN'S**
123 Lexington Avenue
New York, NY 10016
212.685.3451
www.kalustyans.com

**PARIS GOURMET**
145 Grand Street
Carlstadt, NJ 07072
201.939.5656
800.727.8791
www.parisgourmet.com

## Baking Equipment: Small Tools, Large Equipment

**BROADWAY PANHANDLER**
65 East 8th Street
New York, NY 10003
212.966.3434
www.broadwaypanhandler.com

**INSTANT WARES**
www.instawares.com

**JB PRINCE COMPANY**
36 East 31st Street
New York, NY 10016
212.683.3553
www.jbprince.com

**KEREKES BAKERY & RESTAURANT EQUIPMENT INC.**
6103 15th Avenue
Brooklyn, NY 11219
1.800.525.5556
www.bakedeco.com

## Cookie Cutters

**COPPER GIFTS**
900 N. 32nd Street
Parsons, KS 67357
866.898.3965
www.CopperGifts.com

IND